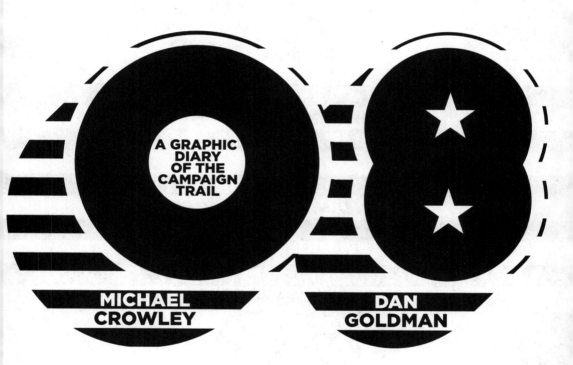

08

A GRAPHIC DIARY OF THE CAMPAIGN TRAIL

MICHAEL CROWLEY

DAN GOLDMAN

OTHER BOOKS BY
DAN GOLDMAN:

SHOOTING WAR
EVERYMAN: BE THE PEOPLE

Published in the United States by Three
Rivers Press, an imprint of the
Crown Publishing Group, a division of
Random House, Inc., New York.

www.crownpublishing.com

Three Rivers Press and the Tugboat design
are registered trademarks of
Random House, Inc.

Library of Congress
Cataloging-in-Publication Data
is available upon request.

ISBN 978-0-307-40511-1

Printed in the United States of America

Illustrated by Dan Goldman
Drawn on Wacom Cintiq
Author photos by Seth Kushner

10 9 8 7 6 5 4 3 2 1
First Edition

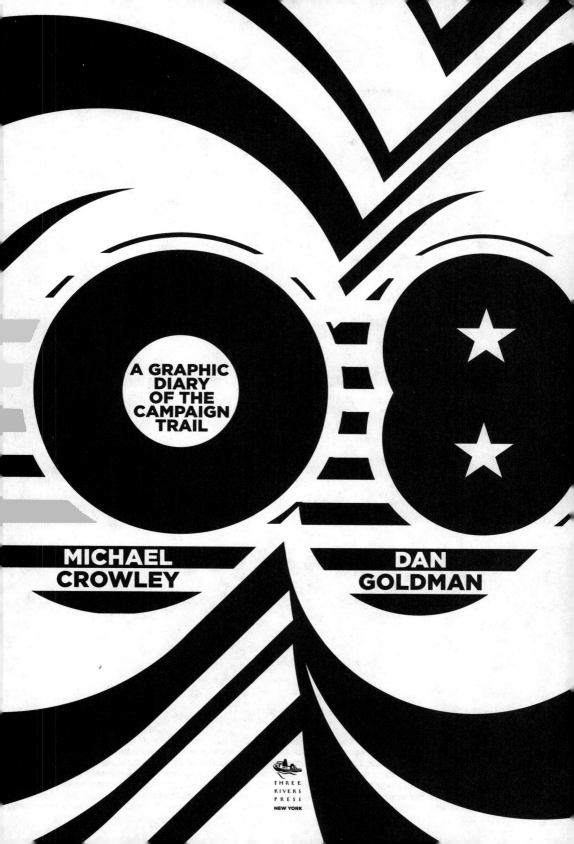

A GRAPHIC
DIARY
OF THE
CAMPAIGN
TRAIL

MICHAEL CROWLEY

DAN GOLDMAN

THREE
RIVERS
PRESS
NEW YORK

2006

THE 2006 ELECTIONS MARKED
THE END OF THE REPUBLICAN ERA.

FOR SIX YEARS, WASHINGTON HAD BEEN DOMINATED BY **GEORGE W. BUSH, DICK CHENEY, AND TOM DELAY.**

AFTER 9/11 IT SEEMED LIKE THE GOP MIGHT RULE AMERICA **FOREVER.**

UNTIL EVERYTHING

WENT OFF THE RAILS.

JACK ABRAMOFF

AMERICA HAD OFFICIALLY GIVEN BUSH THE FINGER

RUNNING FOR PRESIDENT AS A REPUBLICAN WAS NOT GOING TO BE FUN.

BUT JOHN MCCAIN HAD SEEN WORSE.

IN 1967, LT. CMDR. JOHN McCAIN WAS SHOT DOWN OVER VIETNAM AND TAKEN PRISONER.

HE SPENT THE NEXT FIVE YEARS THERE AS A P.O.W.

DEFIANT, AND BRUTALLY BEATEN FOR IT,

HE WOULD NEVER RAISE HIS ARMS ABOVE HIS HEAD AGAIN.

THE SON OF ADMIRAL JOHN S. McCAIN JR.

McCAIN WAS OFFERED EARLY RELEASE.

BUT HE REFUSED TO LEAVE BEFORE OTHERS WHO'D BEEN THERE LONGER. IT WAS A MATTER OF HONOR.

SOMEHOW HE MADE IT HOME ALIVE...

★★ AND WENT INTO POLITICS. ★★

HE STARTED OUT AS A HARD CONSERVATIVE PROTÉGÉ OF BARRY GOLD-WATER AND BOOSTER OF RONALD REAGAN.

THE 1989 KEATING FIVE SCANDAL NEARLY ENDED HIS CAREER.

BUT HE REMADE HIMSELF, MAKING A NAME AS A "MAVERICK" WHO TOOK ON HIS OWN PARTY.

HE PUSHED FOR CAMPAIGN FINANCE REFORM LAWS CONSERVATIVES HATED.

FOUGHT BIG TOBACCO TO THE DEATH.

...AND INFURIATED HIS SENATE COLLEAGUES BY CALLING OUT THEIR PORK-BARREL SPENDING.

STILL, THE PRESS ADORED HIM. HE WAS FUNNY, IRONIC. THEY COULDN'T GET ENOUGH OF HIS "STRAIGHT TALK."

BY 2000, HE WAS A POLITICAL STAR. ENOUGH TO RUN FOR PRESIDENT. ENOUGH TO BEAT GEORGE W. BUSH IN THE NEW HAMPSHIRE PRIMARY. THERE ALMOST WAS NO BUSH PRESIDENCY.

2007

IN THE BEGINNING, ALL EYES WERE ON **ONE WOMAN.**

AS FIRST LADY HILLARY CLINTON HAD BEEN **ONE OF THE MOST REVILED FIGURES** IN AMERICAN POLITICS.

BUT WHEN BILL LEFT THE WHITE HOUSE IN 2000, SHE RAN FOR SENATE IN NEW YORK —

A STATE WHERE SHE'D NEVER EVEN LIVED.

AND SHE PULLED IT OFF.

OF COURSE, IT WAS NEVER REALLY ABOUT **NEW YORK.**

IT WAS A **STEPPING STONE** TO THE OVAL OFFICE.

THEY HAD BIG MONEY.

PEOPLE ALL OVER WASHINGTON.

DEMOCRATS ADORED BILL.

BUT PLENTY OF PEOPLE SIMPLY DIDN'T TRUST HILLARY.

ONE BIG REASON: THE IRAQ WAR.

SEN. HILLARY CLINTON

> This is probably the hardest decision I have ever had to make — any vote that may lead to war should be hard — but I cast it with conviction.

...SHE STUCK WITH BUSH ON THE OCCUPATION AFTER OTHER DEMOCRATS BAILED OUT.

> Now that we're [in Iraq], we have no choice. We own this issue.

> There is no doubt that we're going to be there for years...

> Whether you agreed or not that we should be in Iraq, failure is not an option.

SEN. ROBERT KERREY

THE LEFT WANTED SOMEONE WHO'D STOOD UP, SPOKEN OUT. THE OLD HOWARD DEAN CROWD WASN'T ABOUT TO SUPPORT HILLARY.

AND THEY DEFINITELY DIDN'T WANT *HIM* BACK.

OTHER DEMOCRATS CAME FORWARD:

RICHARDSON

BIDEN

DODD

AND DON'T **FORGET** KUCINICH.

HE WAS ALWAYS GOOD FOR A LAUGH.

AND JOHN EDWARDS...?

NO ONE REALLY BLAMED HIM FOR 2004.

IOWA

SO HE JUST NEVER STOPPED RUNNING.

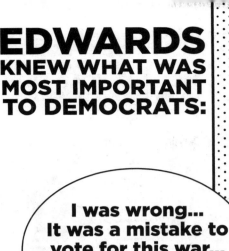

EDWARDS KNEW WHAT WAS MOST IMPORTANT TO DEMOCRATS:

I was wrong... It was a mistake to vote for this war... I take responsibility for that mistake.

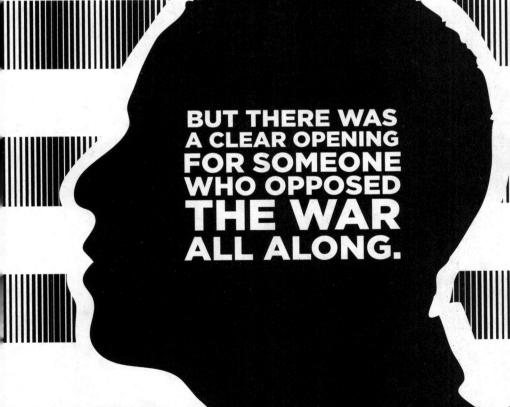

BUT THERE WAS A CLEAR OPENING FOR SOMEONE WHO OPPOSED THE WAR ALL ALONG.

OBAMA'S STORY BEGAN WITH A FOREIGN EXCHANGE STUDENT FROM KENYA WHO CAME TO HAWAII IN 1961 AND MET A 17-YEAR-OLD KANSAS GIRL NAMED ANN DUNHAM.

INTERRACIAL COUPLES WERE STILL TABOO IN MUCH OF AMERICA. BUT THEY MARRIED, HAD A BABY. THEY NAMED HIM BARACK HUSSEIN OBAMA, AFTER HIS FATHER.

BUT BARACK SR. WOULDN'T STAY LONG. HE LEFT TO STUDY AT HARVARD, AND RETURNED TO KENYA SOON AFTER.

YOUNG "BARRY" BOUNCED AROUND: ANN DUNHAM FOLLOWED A NEW MAN TO INDONESIA, WHERE BARRY SAW ANOTHER WORLD.

AS A TEENAGER HE WAS A POPULAR HOOPS STAR. BUT MAYBE NOT A MODEL YOUTH.

GIVING UP "BARRY" FOR HIS FATHER'S FULL NAME, OBAMA STUDIED AT COLUMBIA, THEN WENT TO HARVARD LAW SCHOOL, WHERE PEOPLE **RECOGNIZED HIM AS A STAR.**

LONG TORN BETWEEN THE BLACK AND WHITE WORLDS, HE FOUND A HOME IN CHICAGO — FIRST AS A **COMMUNITY ORGANIZER,** THEN AS A LAW **PROFESSOR.**

HE FOUND A WIFE, AND A SPIRITUAL HOME IN A BLACK CHURCH, WHERE THE MINISTER PREACHED OF THE **"AUDACITY TO HOPE."**

I NOW... PRONOUNCE YOU...

MAN AND WIFE!!!

IN 1996 OBAMA BEGAN A POLITICAL CAREER, WINNING A HYDE PARK STATE SENATE SEAT.

ELECT **Dave Koehle State Sena** 46th Dis

BUT HE WOULD LOSE HIS MOTHER **SOON AFTER.** HIS FATHER HAD **DIED IN KENYA** YEARS BEFORE.

A RUN FOR CONGRESS IN 2000 DIDN'T WORK OUT AS WELL.

BUT A FEW YEARS LATER, **A RETIREMENT IN WASHINGTON** OPENED THE DOOR TO HIS FUTURE.

AND TO AMERICA'S **FUTURE.**

EIGHT YEARS AFTER HIS FIRST RUN, JOHN McCAIN WAS READY TO TRY AGAIN. BUT THIS TIME HE WOULD DO THINGS DIFFERENTLY.

BACK IN 2000, McCAIN HAD RUN AGAINST THE **REPUBLICAN PARTY'S CONSERVATIVE BASE.**

Neither party should be defined by pandering to the outer reaches of American politics and the agents of intolerance...

...whether they be Louis Farrakhan and Al Sharpton on the left, or Pat Robertson or Jerry Falwell on the right.

BUT THAT CAMPAIGN TAUGHT HIM A LESSON: YOU DON'T WIN A REPUBLICAN PRIMARY THAT WAY.

I believe that the "Christian Right" has a major role to play in the Republican Party. One reason is because they're so active and their followers are.

And I believe they have a right to be a part of our party. I don't have to agree with everything they stand for.

HE MADE PEACE WITH OLD ENEMIES.

FLIP-FLOPPED ON THE BUSH TAX CUTS.

GAVE CREDENCE TO CREATIONISM.

IN SHORT, THE ONE-TIME REBEL BECAME THE ESTABLISHMENT CANDIDATE.
AND THE NOMINATION WAS MCCAIN'S TO LOSE.

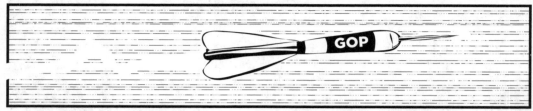

EVEN IF PLENTY OF REPUBLICANS WEREN'T READY TO FORGIVE HIS HERESIES.

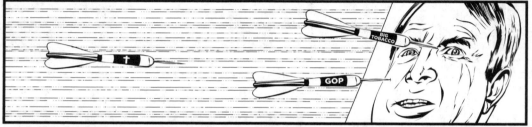

MCCAIN DID GET ONE LUCKY BREAK.

VIRGINIA SENATOR GEORGE ALLEN WAS SUPPOSED TO BE THE "CONSERVATIVE" CANDIDATE AND A TOUGH RIVAL.

UNTIL HE HAD ONE OF THE MOST SPECTACULAR MELTDOWNS EVER...

...CONCERNING AN INDIAN-AMERICAN FILMING HIS SPEECH FOR OPPONENT JIM WEBB'S CAMPAIGN.

Let's give a welcome to *macaca** here. Welcome to America, and the real world.

S.R. SIDARTH

04:49

GEORGE ALLEN 'MACACA' CAREER-ENDING GAFF

THROW IN STORIES ABOUT HIS LOVE OF THE N-WORD, AND THAT WAS THE END OF HIM.

*MONKEY

BUT McCAIN FACED OTHER TOUGH FOES.

9/11 TURNED RUDY GIULIANI INTO AN AMERICAN ICON, BUT HE ARRIVED LOADED WITH BAGGAGE: THREE MARRIAGES UNDER HIS BELT...

...AND HIS, ER, *FABULOUS* PERSONA AS NEW YORK MAYOR.

AND THEN THE $64,000 QUESTION:

COULD SOMEONE WHO DOESN'T CONSIDER ABORTION MURDER BE THE REPUBLICAN NOMINEE?

HOW FAR COULD THE MEMORY OF 9/11 TAKE HIM?

THEN THERE WAS MITT ROMNEY, A REPUBLICAN WHO'D GOTTEN ELECTED GOVERNOR OF LIBERAL MASSACHUSETTS.

ROMNEY HAD A LOT GOING FOR HIM, TOO: SMART, GOOD-LOOKING. SUCCESSFUL BUSINESSMAN. RAN THE 2002 OLYMPICS,

AND A FORTUNE OF $250 MILLION.

BUT GETTING ELECTED IN MASSACHUSETTS MEANT THAT ROMNEY HAD SAID SOME INCONVENIENT THINGS:

WILL I PRESERVE AND PROTECT A WOMAN'S RIGHT TO CHOOSE? YES.

I DON'T LINE UP WITH THE NRA.

WE MUST MAKE EQUALITY FOR GAYS AND LESBIANS A MAINSTREAM CONCERN.

AND THEN THERE WAS THE ELEPHANT IN THE ROOM: WAS AMERICA READY FOR A MORMON PRESIDENT?

A FEW OTHER SINGLE-ISSUE CANDIDATES JUMPED INTO THE RACE.

SO DID AN OBSCURE LIBERTARIAN NAMED **RON PAUL, WHO ARGUED THAT THE GOP HAD ABANDONED ITS CORE PRINCIPLES.**

HE WAS FUNNY-LOOKING AND A TERRIBLE SPEAKER. BUT HE WAS AN OUTSIDER — AND THAT TOUCHED A NERVE.

A BIGGER ONE THAN ANYBODY COULD HAVE PREDICTED.

AS THE CAMPAIGN GOT ROLLING IN 2007, THE ESTABLISHMENT CANDIDATE **WAS LOOKING SHAKY.** THE FEISTY MAVERICK WAS **NOW 71, AND IT SHOWED.** HE SEEMED TIRED, GRUMPY.

HIS ADAMANT SUPPORT FOR THE WAR WAS BURNING UP HIS CREDIBILITY.

AFTER ONE TRIP TO IRAQ HE CLAIMED THAT AN AMERICAN COULD "WALK FREELY" THROUGH A BAGHDAD MARKET.

NOT QUITE.

HE NEVER BACKED AWAY FROM THE WAR.

BUT THAT DIDN'T STOP CONSERVATIVES FROM TURNING ON HIM.

NOTHING DROVE THE RIGHT WING CRAZY LIKE *ILLEGAL IMMIGRATION*.

MCCAIN HAD EVEN WORKED WITH TED KENNEDY ON A BILL THAT WOULD ALLOW SOME ILLEGAL IMMIGRANTS TO BECOME CITIZENS.

This is the Destroy the Republican Party Act.

ALL THE OLD ANGER AT MCCAIN CAME BACK, AND HIS FUND-RAISING **DRIED UP.**

BY SUMMER, **HE WAS BROKE.**

HE BLAMED HIS **TOP STAFF.**

STUNNED AND **BETRAYED,** HE EVEN FIRED JOHN WEAVER, ONE OF HIS OLDEST **FRIENDS AND TOP ADVISORS.**

A FLOOD OF OTHER AIDES **QUIT OR** WERE FIRED.

MCCAIN WAS **BANKRUPT. HUMILIATED.**

CHARLIE COOK

> For all intents and purposes, McCain's campaign is over. The physicians have pulled up the sheet; the executors of the estate are taking over.

> I'm only still here in case he drops out.

> I feel your pain.

BUT MCCAIN JUST WOULDN'T QUIT.

HE'D BEEN THROUGH WORSE.

JUST AS THE WAR WAS DEFINING MCCAIN, SO IT DEFINED ANOTHER MAN.

I don't oppose all wars. What I am opposed to is a dumb war. What I am opposed to is a rash war.

What I am opposed to is the cynical attempt by Richard Perle and Paul Wolfowitz and other armchair, weekend warriors in this administration to shove their own ideological agendas down our throats, irrespective of the costs in lives lost and in hardships borne.

OCTOBER 2002

NOVEMBER 2005

I can unequivocally say I will not be running for national office in four years.

OCTOBER 2006

I don't want to be coy about this... I have thought about the possibility.

I recognize there is a certain presumptuousness, a certain audacity, to this announcement....

JANUARY 2007

In the face of war, you believe there can be peace. In the face of despair, you believe there can be hope.

In the face of a politics that's shut you out, that's told you to settle, that's divided us for too long...

...you believe we can be one people, reaching for what's possible, building that more perfect union.

It is clear that we need to change our strategy in Iraq... Failure in Iraq would be a *disaster* for the United States.

THIS TALK OF HOPE CAME AT AN ESPECIALLY HOPELESS TIME.

IRAQ WAS A NONSTOP **BLOODBATH.** BUT BUSH ORDERED A TROOP SURGE...

...EVEN AS MOST AMERICANS JUST WANTED *OUT*.

DEMOCRATS WERE HARDLY IN A MOOD TO FORGIVE HILLARY FOR HER VOTE.

I want to know if right here, right now, once and for all and without nuance, you can say that war authorization was a mistake...

Until we hear you say it, we're not going to hear all the other great things you are saying.

Knowing what I know now, I would never have voted for it...

(BUT SHE NEVER ACTUALLY APOLOGIZED.)

JOHN EDWARDS STAKED OUT THE LEFT WING.
HE CAST HIMSELF AS A LIBERAL VOICE OF CONSCIENCE, A CHAMPION OF THE LITTLE GUY, AN ANTI-POVERTY CRUSADER.

SOME PEOPLE CALLED HIM A HYPOCRITE...

IT WAS NOTHING
COMPARED TO THIS:

My wife's cancer is back.

SOMETIMES YOU GOTTA PLAY THE HAND LIFE DEALS YOU.

Senator Edwards... what does this mean for your campaign?

The campaign goes on.

AND WHILE SOME PEOPLE WONDERED HOW HE COULD KEEP RUNNING...

The campaign goes on *strongly*.

OBAMAMANIA WAS GOING VIRAL.

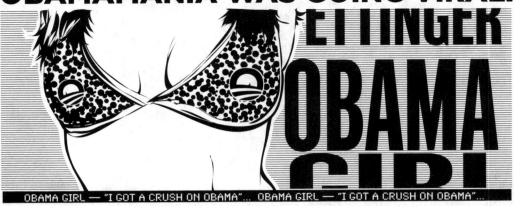

OBAMA GIRL — "I GOT A CRUSH ON OBAMA"... OBAMA GIRL — "I GOT A CRUSH ON OBAMA"...

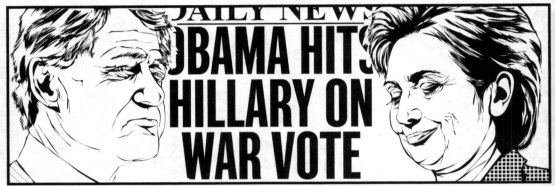

THE CLINTONS HADN'T PREPARED FOR THIS,
AND IT DROVE THEM CRAZY...

Hillary is the most experienced candidate I will ever have had the chance to vote for.

IT WAS AS THOUGH THE NOMINATION BELONGED TO THEM.
ONLY HILLARY HAD THE "EXPERIENCE"
TO BE PRESIDENT, THEY SAID.

HOW SO WAS ALWAYS A LITTLE VAGUE.

HILLARY ALSO TACKED LEFT ON THE WAR. BY MARCH 2007 SHE WAS CALLING FOR MOST TROOPS OUT OF IRAQ.

If we in Congress don't end this war before January 2009...

...as president, *I will.*

BILL INSISTED OBAMA'S DIFFERENCES WITH HILLARY WERE OVER-BLOWN.

This dichotomy that's been set up to allow him to become the raging hero of the anti-war crowd on the Internet is just *factually inaccurate.*

BUT BY SPRING 2007 SHE WAS CLEARLY IN TROUBLE.

THE DEBATES **BEGIN:** GAME ON.

THE DEBATES WERE SOMETHING OF A CIRCUS, TO BE SURE.

FOR INSTANCE, WHO DECIDED MIKE GRAVEL BELONGED UP THERE?

EVERYONE AGREED: HILLARY ACED THE EARLY DEBATES.

EVEN CONSERVATIVE PUNDITS
WERE SMITTEN.

OBAMA WAS AMAZING BEFORE A CROWD. BUT THE SMALLER STAGE DIMINISHED HIM.

HE WAS LESS INSPIRATIONAL THAN... PROFESSORIAL.

The federal law is not being enforced not because of failures of local communities, but because the federal government has not done the job that it needs to do.

SOME OF THESE EARLY STUMP SPEECHES WERE REAL SNOOZERS.

And —

Erm...

HILLARY, MEANWHILE, WAS A MACHINE. SHE NEVER SEEMED TO MAKE A MISTAKE.

DISDAINFUL OF ATTACK POLITICS, OBAMA TRIED TO **KEEP THINGS POSITIVE.** TOO POSITIVE, SOME SAID. THEY WONDERED IF HE COULD GO FOR THE JUGULAR.

He has got to attack and he has got to explain why Hillary Clinton cannot win the presidency. And that she can't govern because she will divide the country.

It is a tough thing for him to do but he has got to do it. He is a lawyer but he has a judicial temperament, not a prosecutorial temperament.

Well said.

HOWARD FINEMAN

PEOPLE WONDERED IF THEY WERE SEEING A REPEAT OF HISTORY.

HUGE CROWDS AND MEDIA **HYPE** THAT WOULD END IN A **FIZZLE.**

OBAMA WAS STALLED IN THE POLLS. HIS TOP SUPPORTERS WERE ANTSY.

The Republicans are obsessed with you, Hillary. It is the fight that we've been through since the '90s.

The next president's job is to break the gridlock and get Democrats and independents and Republicans working together to solve these big problems.

SURE, HE'D TAKE HIS SHOTS AT HER FROM TIME TO TIME.

LIKE WHEN HILLARY CAST A SENATE VOTE TO GET TOUGH ON IRAN.

Her willingness to once again extend the president the benefit of the doubt shows that she hasn't fully learned the lessons of 2002.

BUT IT WAS EDWARDS WHO HIT HER THE HARDEST:

Senator Clinton's road to the middle class takes a *major detour* right through the deep canyon of corporate lobbyists and the hidden bidding of K Street in Washington.

NOTHING SEEMED TO STICK TO HILLARY, THOUGH.

BY OCTOBER OF 2007, HILLARY SEEMED UNSTOPPABLE.

ON THE GOP SIDE, MCCAIN'S COLLAPSE HAD LEFT A VACUUM. ON THE ONE HAND, RUDY WAS ROMPING THE NATIONAL POLLS.

(THANK YOU, 9/11)

AT THE SAME TIME, ROMNEY WAS BLASTING THE EARLY PRIMARY STATES WITH EXPENSIVE AD BUYS.

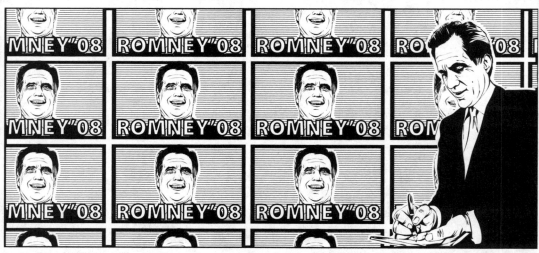

AND BEFORE YOU COULD SAY "BUYING THE ELECTION," MITT WAS THE FRONT-RUNNER IN IOWA AND NEW HAMPSHIRE.

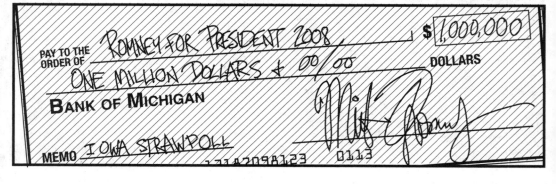

AND SO ON SEPTEMBER 5, 2007,
FRED THOMPSON'S CANDIDACY WAS BORN.

FITTINGLY FOR AN ACTOR...

...HE DID IT ON A TV SHOW.

AS FRED GOT HIS ACT TOGETHER,
ROMNEY AND RUDY WENT AT IT OVER
WHO WAS MORE CONSERVATIVE.

BUT THIS HUCKABEE GUY WAS
CATCHING ON IN IOWA.

FOR DEMOCRATS, EVERYTHING CHANGED AT AN OCTOBER 30 DEBATE IN PHILADELPHIA.

IT BEGAN AS ANOTHER STRONG NIGHT FOR HILLARY, ANOTHER FLAT ONE FOR OBAMA.

He has a health care plan that doesn't cover *every American.*

My plan does. It is a *defining* contrast.

It was unidentified flying object, okay. It's like—it's unidentified. I saw something.

AT FIRST THE MAIN EVENT WAS DENNIS KUCINICH'S CLAIM THAT HE'D ONCE SEEN A UFO.

BUT IN THE CLOSING MINUTES OF THE DEBATE, TIM RUSSERT ASKED HILLARY ABOUT HER PAST SUPPORT FOR A NEW YORK PLAN TO GIVE DRIVER'S LICENSES TO ILLEGAL **IMMIGRANTS.**

IN OLD-SCHOOL CLINTON FASHION, **SHE TRIED TO HAVE IT BOTH WAYS.**

I did not say that it should be done, but I certainly recognize why Governor Spitzer is trying to do it.

Wait a minute! No, no, no.

You said *yes,* you thought *it made sense to do it.*

SUDDENLY **BLOOD** WAS IN THE **WATER.**

IT WOULD PROVE A MAJOR TURNING POINT.

THE BAD OLD **HILLARY WAS BACK:** CALCULATING, SAYING ANYTHING TO GET AHEAD.

Uh-oh...

It's about time.

Newsday
NEW YORK CITY

THE HEAT'S ON HILLARY

FOR THE FIRST — BUT HARDLY THE LAST — TIME, **SHE PLAYED THE VICTIM CARD.**

HER TEAM WARNED THAT SHE'D BEEN THE VICTIM **OF A "PILE-ON"** THAT WOULD CAUSE **A BACKLASH AMONG WOMEN.**

BUT SOMETHING HAD CHANGED FOR GOOD. HILLARY'S PERFECT FAÇADE WAS SHATTERED.

Two months till the Iowa caucuses, Harlan.

Time to hit the trail.

LADIES AND GENTLEMEN PLE
YOUR SAFETY BELTS AND
THE UPRIGHT POS
DESCENT IN

THE IOWA CAUCUS

FOR ALL THE HYPE, FRED'S DEBUT ON THE TRAIL WAS ...UNDERWHELMING.

IT TURNED OUT THAT PEOPLE WERE MORE INTERESTED IN A *LAW AND ORDER* ACTOR THAN A CANDIDATE.

FRED KEPT A *NOTICEABLY LIGHT* SCHEDULE.

OR IN THE (MUCH YOUNGER) WOMAN AT HIS SIDE.

DURING PEAK PRIMARY SEASON HE WAS EVEN SPOTTED *SHOPPING.*

IN VIRGINIA.

THOMPSON'S FIZZLE WAS GREAT NEWS FOR RUDY.
EVEN THOUGH HE WAS TANKING IN IOWA AND NEW HAMPSHIRE,
"AMERICA'S MAYOR" WAS STILL THE NATIONAL FRONT-RUNNER.

SO RUDY CAMPAIGNED LIKE HE WAS ALREADY THE NOMINEE.

THAT MEANT TOUGH TALK ON IMMIGRATION... AND TERRORISM.

RUDY COULD TURN ANYTHING INTO A QUESTION ABOUT HOMELAND SECURITY.

What would you do if--

--if something living on another planet comes over here?

That's the first time I've been asked how we're going to prepare for an outer space attack.

But if we're properly prepared for all the different things that can happen to us, we'll be prepared for that as well.

THAT WAS ENOUGH TO MAKE HIM SOME VERY IMPORTANT FRIENDS.

PAT ROBERTSON

To me, the overriding issue before the American people --

-- is the defense of our population from the bloodlust of Islamic terrorists.

BUT RUDY HAD SOME VERY BIG PROBLEMS, TOO.

"Giuliani ally hit with tax evasion, corruption charges."

The company you keep...

NEW YORK OBSERVER
KERIK INDICTED

POLITICO

Giuliani billed obscure agencies for trips

By BEN SMITH   11/28/07 2:47 PM EST Updated: 11/30/07 11:33 AM

IN THE EARLY NOVEMBER DAYS FOLLOWING HER DEBATE FIASCO, EVERYTHING SEEMED TO GO SOUR FOR HILLARY.

LIKE WHEN NPR REPORTED SHE HADN'T LEFT A TIP AFTER VISITING A TOLEDO, IOWA **RESTAURANT.**

THE STORY WAS FALSE. AND HILLARY'S AIDES WERE **MORE CONVINCED THAN EVER THAT THE PRESS WAS OUT TO GET HER.**

A FEW DAYS LATER:

TURNS OUT THE QUESTION WAS PLANTED.

HILLARY HELD HER BIG LEAD IN NATIONAL POLLS. BUT SHE WAS SLIPPING IN IOWA.

She shoulda just skipped the caucuses and gone right to New Hampshire.

Remember, they thought about it.

SHE IGNORED THAT ADVICE.

INTERNAL MEMO
FROM: Mike Henry
TO: HRC

I propose skipping the Iowa caucuses and dedicating more of Senator Clinton's time and financial resources on the primary in New Hampshire on January 22, the Nevada caucus on January 19, primaries in South Carolina and Florida on January 29 and the 20 plus state primaries on February 5th.

BUT WHEN OBAMA OUTSHONE HILLARY BEFORE A HUGE CROWD AT A NOVEMBER 7 EVENT IN DES MOINES, THAT DECISION SEEMED QUESTIONABLE.

THIS WAS THE OBAMA PEOPLE HAD SEEN AT THE 2004 CONVENTION.

America, our moment is now. Our moment is now.

I am not in this race to fulfill some long-held ambitions or because I believe it's somehow owed to me.

I never expected to be here. I always knew this journey was improbable. I've never been on a journey that wasn't.

Gee, wonder who he's talking about...

Ha! You should totally blog that.

I am running in this race because of what Dr. King called "the fierce urgency of now."

Because I believe that there's such a thing as being too late. And that hour is almost upon us.

God, he's good...

IOWANS OF ALL STRIPES WERE ENCHANTED.

I haven't felt this way since Bobby Kennedy.

Bro, where do I register?

STOP. WARS

BEER

Obama's people look like *Facebook*.

Only a few of their people looked old enough to vote.

AND THE CLINTON TEAM WAS LEFT SOUNDING LIKE GRUMPY OLD PEOPLE.

ON THE GOP SIDE, DECEMBER OPENED WITH AN EARTHQUAKE.

THE CHRISTIAN CONSERVATIVES WHO DOMINATE THE IOWA REPUBLICAN PARTY DIDN'T TRUST THE LIKES OF RUDY, MCCAIN, OR MITT.

THEY FLOCKED TO THE EVANGELICAL PASTOR FROM ARKANSAS.

CHRISTIAN LEADER

HUCK'S ADS WERE BLUNT ABOUT HIS "QUALIFICATIONS."

BUT UNLIKE MOST RELIGIOUS CONSERVATIVES,

HUCK HAD AN **EDGE:**

REAL MEDIA-PLEASING GIMMICKS.

PLUS, EVERYONE ALWAYS LOVES AN UNDERDOG.

NEVER MIND THAT HUCK DIDN'T HAVE A CLUE ABOUT FOREIGN POLICY.

AS THE MAJOR CANDIDATES FOUGHT IT OUT, SOMETHING STRANGE WAS HAPPENING UNDER THE RADAR.

IGNORED BY THE MAJOR MEDIA, RON PAUL'S ANTI-WAR, LIBERTARIAN MESSAGE WAS DRAWING MILLIONS OF FOLLOWERS ONLINE.

NEVER MIND THAT PAUL HIMSELF BARELY KNEW HOW TO USE A COMPUTER.

The Internet is delightful for finding the information, and if there's a question that I need, ask, you can find it.

AND THE WACKIER HE SOUNDED TO MAINSTREAM EARS...

Abolish the Federal Reserve!

They're planning on millions of acres taken by eminent domain for an international highway from Mexico to Canada.

Our national sovereignty is *under threat.*

The Trilateral Commission *exists.* And it's a, quote, "conspiracy of ideas."

...THE MORE HIS PEOPLE LOVED HIM.

POLL: THREE-WAY TIE IN IOWA

BY DECEMBER, THE DEMOCRATIC RACE **WAS A TOSS-UP. BIDEN, DODD, AND RICHARDSON JUST HADN'T CAUGHT ON. IT WAS DOWN TO** HILLARY AND OBAMA — AND EDWARDS, WHO **WAS HANGING TOUGH, FIRING UP LIBERALS WITH A POPULIST MESSAGE ON IRAQ, HEALTH CARE, AND THE ECONOMY.**

There's *no excuse* for politicians in Washington to have health care when America doesn't have health care.

I was born in a small town...

JOHN MELLENCAMP HELPED REMIND PEOPLE OF EDWARDS' ROOTS.

ELIZABETH WAS A STAR IN HER OWN RIGHT.

THEY SURE SEEMED LIKE A LOVING COUPLE.

AND THERE WERE MORE SERIOUS DOUBTS.

RIELLE HUNTER

Look directly into the lens, John... er, *Senator.*

IT WAS OBAMA WHO HAD THE REAL MOMENTUM.

AND HILLARYLAND WAS PANICKING.

I know he is the one.

DETERMINED NOT TO LOSE IOWA, SHE WENT NEGATIVE.

Voters will judge whether living in a foreign country at the age of ten prepares one to face the big, complex international challenges the next president will face.

I think we need a president with more *experience* than that.

How did *running for president* become a qualification for *being president?*

Some believe you get change by *hoping for it.* I believe you get it by *working hard.*

SHE TRIED TO TURN OBAMAMANIA AGAINST HIM, SAYING HE WAS ALL TALK, NO ACTION.

HER TEAM WENT TO ABSURD EXTREMES.

Now she's going after things he said *in kindergarten?*

...n kindergarten
...Senator Obama
...y titled 'I
...ec..ne Presiden
...armawan, 63, S
...ama's kinderg
...cher, remembe..
...n exceptionally
...curly haired ch
...quickly picked
...ocal language a
...harp math skil
...rote an essay ti
...nt To Become
...ent,' the teache
...[AP, 1/25/07]

ONE TOP HILLARY BACKER
WARNED THAT REPUBLICANS WOULD **ATTACK OBAMA FOR HIS PAST COKE USE.**

Cocaine... cocaine...

He- He just *said it again!*

HARDBALL
OBAMA ADMITS COCAINE USE

MARK PENN KEPT THE
STORY ALIVE ON *HARDBALL.*

THE MESSAGE: OBAMA HAS SKELETONS IN HIS CLOSET.

I've been tested, I've been vetted. There are no surprises.... We need to nominate a candidate who *can win.*

BILL GOT IN ON THE ACT, TOO.

When is the last time we elected a president based on one year of service in the Senate before he started running?... The Obama people got the press on their side.

We're prepared to roll the dice.

Rolling the dice about America?

It's less predictable, isn't it?

Bill Clinton
Former U.S. President

The real gamble in this election is playing the *same Washington game* with the *same Washington players* and expecting a *different result.*

And that's a risk we *can't* take.

RESERVED FOR PRESS

ROAD TO CHANGE

I see him!! Here he comes!!

I see *trees,* I see *snow...* but I don't see no *high school...*

WITH MOST OF THE ACTION CONCENTRATED IN IOWA, MCCAIN WAS FLYING UNDER THE RADAR IN NEW HAMPSHIRE.

NEARLY BROKE, HE SKIPPED THE IOWA CIRCUS ALTOGETHER, PUTTING HIS EGGS IN THE BASKET OF NEW HAMPSHIRE'S JANUARY 8 VOTE.

RUNNING ON FUMES, MCCAIN NEEDED A $3 MILLION LOAN JUST TO KEEP HIS CAMPAIGN ALIVE.

HE'D EVEN DOWNGRADED HIS "STRAIGHT TALK EXPRESS" BUS TO A CHEAPER MODEL, DUBBED THE "NO SURRENDER" BUS.

BUT MCCAIN HAD SOMETHING GOING FOR HIM THAT MONEY CAN'T BUY: HE WAS A GREAT CAMPAIGNER. HE SAID UNEXPECTED THINGS.

I promise you, my friends, I'll close Guantanamo Bay and we will *never torture another person* in our custody again.

WHEN PROTESTERS SHOWED UP AT HIS EVENTS, HE DIDN'T RUN FROM THEM...

You, sir — Do you have a question?

...HE CALLED ON THEM.

And that, my friends, is a little straight talk!

HE'D SIT ON HIS BUS AND TALK TO REPORTERS FOR HOURS.

THEY COULDN'T GET ENOUGH OF HIM.

HE COULD EVEN BE A LITTLE LOOPY.

You look kind of dorky in that hat.

Do you worry that you might die in office...

...or get Alzheimer's?

Thanks for the question, you little jerk.

You're *drafted*.

(AGE WAS A TOUCHY SUBJECT FOR THE 71-YEAR-OLD.)

MOST IMPORTANT, PERHAPS, HE RETOOLED HIS MESSAGE TO PLEASE CONSERVATIVES. TOOK A HARDER LINE ON IMMIGRATION.

I got the message: Americans want the border secure....

The American people want the border secured first. That's what they want. And that's what they're going to get from me.

GAVE NO QUARTER OVER IRAQ.

We must win in Iraq. I repeat, we *must win* in Iraq.

MEANWHILE . . .

THE QUESTION WAS WHETHER HUCK COULD REALLY PULL IT OFF. HE BARELY HAD ANY STAFFERS.

ONE OF THE MOST SENIOR PEOPLE IN THE CAMPAIGN WAS HIS 25 YEAR-OLD DAUGHTER, SARAH.

STILL, ROMNEY'S MILLIONS IN SPENDING HADN'T SLOWED HUCK DOWN.

MITT WAS DESPERATE FOR A WIN HERE TO SHOW THAT HE WAS FOR REAL. BUT THERE WAS SOMETHING A LITTLE TOO PERFECT ABOUT HIM,

AND EVEN HIS FAMILY.

NOT EVERYONE WAS SO IMPRESSED WITH THE ROMNEY BOYS.

HIS RIVALS HAMMERED HIM AS A FLIP-FLOPPER AND A BAD GOVERNOR.

Do they plan to support this war on terrorism by enlisting in our military?

One of the ways my sons are showing support for our nation is helping me to get elected.

Gov. Romney had a very poor record with dealing with murder and violent crime as governor...

...and I think that is not just an isolated situation.

IT DIDN'T DO MUCH FOR LINGERING DOUBTS ABOUT HIS SINCERITY ON ISSUES LIKE IMMIGRATION WHEN HE WAS BUSTED USING ILLEGAL-IMMIGRANT LABORERS AT HIS HOME.

Hola, Señor Romney!

Sigh

AND THE MORMON QUESTION DOGGED HIM. EVEN MCCAIN'S 98-YEAR-OLD MOM GOT INTO THE ACT:

He's a... *MORMON!*

The views of *my mother* are not necessarily the views of mine...

GIVEN THE HUGE INFLUENCE OF EVANGELICAL VOTERS, WHO WERE SUSPICIOUS OF MORMONS, ROMNEY HAD NO OTHER CHOICE.

Almost 50 years ago another candidate from Massachusetts explained that he was an American running for president, not a Catholic running for president. Like him, I am an American running for president. I do not define my candidacy by my religion.

A person should not be elected because of his faith nor should he be rejected because of his faith. Let me assure you that no authorities of my church, or of any other church for that matter, will ever exert influence on presidential decisions.

Yeah, he's Jack Kennedy in 1960.

Give me a break.

Okay, but is Satan Jesus' brother or not?

I think Mike Huckabee is the reason for this speech. Look at those polls.

JOE SCARBOROUGH

WITH MCCAIN WORKING **NEW HAMPSHIRE** AND RUDY VOWING TO **MAKE A STAND** IN FLORIDA AND ON **SUPER TUESDAY ON FEBRUARY 5,**

IOWA WAS COMING DOWN TO A **HUCKABEE-**ROMNEY RACE.

TOM TANCREDO, MEANWHILE, WAS RUNNING SCARY ADS ABOUT IMMIGRATION AND TERRORISTS —

"BECAUSE SOMEBODY **NEEDS TO SAY IT,"** HE EXPLAINED — BUT WAS GOING NOWHERE.

HE WOULD BE OUT OF THE RACE BEFORE CHRISTMAS.

AND FRED NEVER REALLY **STOOD A CHANCE.**

FOR MITT, EVERYTHING WAS RIDING ON WINNING **IOWA.**

IF HE AND HIS MONEY COULDN'T BEAT SOME ARKANSAS **HICK, HOW** COULD ROMNEY POSSIBLY WIN THE NOMINATION?

IT WAS TIME TO GO NEGATIVE.

I think over the coming days as people take a closer look at Governor Huckabee's record, they'll say, "Good guy."

But on matters related to immigration, crime, and spending and taxing, he's too liberal.

ROMNEY HAD SOME POWERFUL ALLIES.

EVEN BUSH'S AMERICA KNEW THEY WOULD **NEVER ELECT** AN EVANGELICAL **PREACHER.**

!!

THE MAN HAD, AFTER ALL, ONCE CALLED FOR QUARANTINING AIDS PATIENTS, AND URGED ONE AUDIENCE TO "TAKE THIS NATION BACK FOR CHRIST."

ECONOMIC CONSERVATIVES PARTICULARLY HATED HIS ANTI-BUSINESS POPULISM.

AND THEN THERE WAS THE BIGGEST DADDY OF THEM ALL.

501-234-0939

Call Mike Huckabee.

Ask why he supported all these taxes.

UNDER ASSAULT, HUCKABEE FIRED BACK AT ROMNEY.

If you get a job by bein dishonest t get it...

...how ca you be trus once you'r that job

IN THE LAST FEW DAYS BEFORE THE CAUCUSES, THE RACE WAS STILL TOO CLOSE TO CALL. THE CANDIDATES RUSHED AROUND THE STATE IN A FRENZY.

CLINTON EVEN FLEW **IN THE HILL-O-COPTER.**

HILLARY'S SUPPORTERS WERE PASSIONATE. BUT OBAMA HAD A FIERCE ORGANIZATION.

HE'D EVEN SIGNED UP THOUSANDS OF HIGH **SCHOOL KIDS.**

HE NEEDED THEM: IOWA WAS DO OR DIE **FOR OBAMA.**

MICHELLE SAID SO HERSELF:

If Barack doesn't win Iowa, then it is just a dream.

BUT THE OLD PROS HAD THEIR DOUBTS ABOUT A BLACK GUY IN CORN COUNTRY.

No one ever won an election counting on the youth vote.

BUT ON CAUCUS DAY, IT WAS CLEAR:

SOMETHING DIFFERENT WAS HAPPENING.

THE CAMPAIGNS WORKED FURIOUSLY TO TURN OUT THEIR SUPPORTERS.

Harlan, Obama got a hell of a turnout over here.

Here at Clintonland, they're acting like they've *already won.*

Holy shit!

FROM JNEWBURY:

OBAMA 37.6,
EDWARDS 29.8,
CLINTON 29.5.

HARDBALL

This is especially tough for Mitt Romney, who outspent Huckabee on television by $6 million...

How do you feel?

Just horrible.

The evangelical base came out, and they all voted for Huckabee.

VIN WEBER

MITT HAD INVESTED **NEARLY** EVERYTHING IN THE EARLY STATES.

AND NOW HE'D LOST THE FIRST CONTEST.

IT WAS ON TO *NEW HAMPSHIRE...*

...WHERE HILLARY'S FUTURE WAS IN DOUBT, TOO.

The worst thing would be to overcount Iowa and its importance. Iowa doesn't have a record of picking presidents.

THE NEW HAMPSHIRE PRIMARY

THE CANDIDATES LANDED IN NEW HAMPSHIRE JUST FOUR DAYS BEFORE THE JANUARY 8 PRIMARY.

(MOST OF THEM: BIDEN AND DODD DIDN'T MAKE IT OUT OF IOWA.)

AND EDWARDS HAD MISSED HIS CHANCE AT BREAKING THROUGH WITH A BIG IOWA UPSET. IT WAS OBAMA PEOPLE WERE WAITING HOURS TO SEE.

JANUARY 20, 2009

First day on the job for the new President

46 million Americans without health care looking for relief...

Global Warming getting worse by the day...

A Prime Minister is on the phone: They've lost a warhead...

How can we be sure the new President is ready?

AND HILLARY WAS ONE MORE LOSS FROM BEING FINISHED.

GROWING DESPERATE, SHE RAMPED UP HER "EXPERIENCE" ARGUMENT.

A DEBATE LOOKED LIKE HER LAST STAND.

What can you say to the voters who seem to like Barack Obama more..?

Well, that hurts my feelings.

He's very likable, but I don't think I'm that bad.

You're likable enough, Hillary.

I've been in *hostage negotiations* that are a lot more civil than this!

ONCE AGAIN, HILLARY CRIED SEXISM.
THE BOYS HAD GANGED UP ON HER AT THE DEBATE. AND THE MALE PUNDITS WERE UNFAIR, TOO, SHE SAID.

Please come on the show.

CHRIS MATTHEWS
MSNBC

YEAH RIGHT.

I just don't know what to do with men who are *obsessed with me.*

HER COMPLAINT WASN'T TOTALLY UNFOUNDED.

A DAY BEFORE THE PRIMARY,
IT LOOKED LIKE HILLARY WAS TOAST...

As a woman I know it's hard to get out of the house and get ready...

...THEN SOMETHING EXTRAORDINARY HAPPENED.

...who does your hair?

It's not easy, it's not easy...

I have so many opportunities for this country. I don't want to see us fall backwards—

This is very personal for me—

—it's not just political, it's not just public.

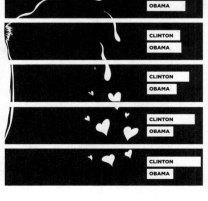

CLINTON
OBAMA

CLINTON
OBAMA

CLINTON
OBAMA

CLINTON
OBAMA

CLINTON
OBAMA

AS THE CLIP LOOPED **ENDLESSLY ON TELEVISION, SOME PEOPLE HAD DOUBTS.**

There were tears that melted the granite state... And those tears clearly moved voters.

But those tears need to be analyzed.

What do you think, Harlan?

I've been doing this too long to think *anything's an accident.*

PRIMARY DAY, JANUARY 8:
ALL THE POLLS SHOWED A BIG OBAMA WIN. REPORTERS STARTED WRITING STORIES ABOUT HILLARY'S DOWNFALL.

TALK OF HILLARY EXIT ENGULFS CAMPAIGN
DRUDGE REPORT

I've already had a few drinks to get me through the night.

Poor guy's out of a job tomorrow.

BUT AS THE DAY WORE ON, IT WAS CLEAR SOMETHING AMAZING WAS HAPPENING.

EXIT POLLS FINAL WAVE: 39-39

39-39.

SOMEHOW, HILLARY HAD PULLED IT OFF, 39-36.

THE RACE WOULD GO ON.

UNLIKE IOWA, THE STATE HAD PRECIOUS **FEW EVANGELICAL VOTERS. HUCK DIDN'T STAND A CHANCE.**

RUDY WAS STILL WAITING IN THE WINGS, **HOPING TO MAKE HIS STAND IN FLORIDA LATER IN THE MONTH. FRED WAS ON LIFE SUPPORT.**

WHILE ROMNEY AND **HUCKABEE HAD BEEN** SLUGGING IT OUT IN IOWA, **MCCAIN HAD BEEN GRINDING AWAY,** HOLDING MORE THAN A HUNDRED TOWN HALLS, **AND STEADILY RISING IN THE POLLS.**

EXETER FOR McCAIN

McCAIN

"John McCain is the man to lead America."

Heh.

THE STATE'S **BIGGEST (AND MOST CONSERVATIVE) PAPER** ENDORSED **HIM — AND** HATED ROMNEY.

If you're not from New Hampshire, you can't appreciate how important a factor [the Union Leader endorsement] is.

They're at DEFCON 5, and it's going to have a significant impact.

SEN. JUDD GREGG

ON ROMNEY

But Romney lacks something John McCain has in spades: conviction. Granite Staters want a candidate who will look them in the eye and tell them the truth. John McCain has done that day in and day out, never wavering, never faltering, never pandering. Mitt Romney has not. He has spoken his lines well, but the people can sense that the words are memorized, not heartfelt.

Zoinks!

MITT TRASHED McCAIN AS A DC HACK AND A **TRAITOR** TO HIS PARTY.

> Senator McCain was one of two Republicans who voted against the Bush tax cuts....

> Don't send us the same people to go to Washington just to fill different chairs and expect change.

> I just wanted to say to Governor Romney, we disagree on a lot of issues...

> ...but I agree you are the *candidate of change.*

FLIP-FLOP

McCAIN USUALLY HAD THE LAST LAUGH.

AND ON PRIMARY **NIGHT**, HE WAS LAUGHING **AGAIN.**

FINAL TALLY:
McCAIN: 37
ROMNEY: 31

> I'd rather have a gold, but I got another silver.

USA!! MACK IS BACK!! USA!! MACK IS BACK!! USA!! MACK IS BACK!! USA!! MACK IS BACK!! USA!! MACK IS BACK!! USA!! MACK IS BACK!! USA!! MACK IS BACK!! USA!! MACK IS BACK!! USA!! MACK

AS THE SHOCK OF HILLARY'S COMEBACK WORE OFF...

Racism. People said they'd vote for Obama...

...but couldn't go through with it.

The thing is, bro:

Working-class voters just don't get the guy.

Javier

Sexism.

THE ANALYSIS BEGAN.

Women know what it's like to catch shit the way she does.

Those *PHONY*

ASS TEARS!

Those *poignant* tears!

NO ONE COULD SAY FOR SURE HOW SHE'D WON. BUT GENDER CLEARLY HAD SOMETHING TO DO WITH IT.

AND AS THE CAMPAIGN MOVED INTO SOUTH CAROLINA, A NEW FACTOR WAS COMING INTO FOCUS: **RACE.**

Bill Clinton is the first black president.

THE CLINTONS WERE ALWAYS BELOVED BY **BLACK AMERICA.**

TONI MORRISON

AT FIRST BLACK VOTERS LOVED HILLARY, AND THEY WEREN'T SURE ABOUT OBAMA

White people will never vote for a black president.

You know somebody's gonna shoot him.

BUT IOWA CHANGED ALL THAT.

IOWA SHOWED THAT EVEN WHITE MIDWESTERNERS WOULD VOTE FOR A BLACK MAN.

CHANGE
WE CAN BELIEVE IN

AT THE SAME TIME, THE CLINTONS WERE STARTING TO SAY THINGS THAT GAVE THEIR OLD ADMIRERS PAUSE.

SOME THOUGHT HILLARY HAD DISSED MLK...

Dr. King's dream began to be realized when President Johnson passed the Civil Rights Act.

It took a president to get it done.

...WHILE BILL SEEMED TO **DIMINISH OBAMA:**

Senator Obama got through 15 debates trumpeting his superior judgment...

There's no difference in his voting record on Iraq and Hillary's. This whole thing is the *biggest fairy tale I've ever seen.*

GIVE. ME. A. BREAK.

The idea that one of these campaigns is positive and the other is negative —

— when I know the reverse is true, and I have seen it —

— is a little tough to take. Just because of the *sanitizing coverage* in the media.

I will tell you, as an African-American, I find his tone and his words to be very depressing.

Now you wait just a cotton-pickin' minute here...

What the hell is racist about that?

AS THE REPUBLICANS HEADED TO MICHIGAN **FOR THE STATE'S** JANUARY 15 PRIMARY.

MCCAIN WAS THE MAN TO BEAT.

MICHIGAN'S ECONOMY WAS IN ROUGH SHAPE.

THE RACE HERE WOULD BE ABOUT POCKETBOOK ISSUES.

I'm aware these are tough times in the heartland of America.

NOT EXACTLY **MCCAIN'S** STRONG SUIT.

I've got to give you some straight talk: Some of the jobs that have left the state of Michigan are *not coming back.*

They are not. And I am sorry to tell you that.

That's a little *too much straight talk...*

WHEREAS MITT WAS MISTER BUSINESS HIMSELF.

Senator McCain said some jobs aren't coming back, I DISAGREE.

I'm going to fight for every single job!!

MICHIGAN WOULD KEEP ROMNEY ALIVE.

Tonight marks the beginning of a comeback!

HE BEAT McCAIN 39-30.

TWO PEOPLE WHO WEREN'T COMING BACK: RUDY AND HUCK.

HIS IOWA MIRACLE **LONG FADED,** HUCKABEE GOT JUST 16 PERCENT, AND WAS NEARLY **BROKE.**

THINGS WERE EVEN WORSE FOR RUDY. HE HADN'T MADE A DENT IN THE EARLY PRIMARIES. HIS NATIONAL POLLING LEAD WAS BLOWN. A FLORIDA UPSET WAS HIS LAST HOPE.

BUT EVEN IN A STATE WHERE HE'D LONG BEEN POPULAR...

...HIZZONER HAD PROBLEMS.

DESPERATE, HE PLAYED HIS FAVORITE CARD.

When the world wavered, and history hesitated, he never did....

Rudy Giuliani. Leadership. When it matters most.

You could probably get a *Law & Order* rerun on TNT there.

Dear Lord have mercy...

BUT THIS PATIENT, TOO, WAS IN CRITICAL CONDITION.

SO WAS MITT, WHO STAYED ON THE OFFENSIVE.

HIS NEW ANGLE: MCCAIN IS TIGHT WITH DC LOBBYISTS.

I don't have lobbyists running my campaign.

What did he just say...?

GLEN JOHNSON

THAT'S *NOT TRUE*, GOVERNOR! THAT IS *NOT TRUE!*

Attaboy! Now *that's* a good reporter!

Panasonic

Now that's *classic Romney.*

RON KAUFMAN, LOBBYIST

ROMNEY DID HAVE SOME TOP AIDES WHO LOBBIED.

NO WONDER ROMNEY'S RIVALS DESPISED HIM.

HUCKABEE'S CAMPAIGN MANAGER CAME OUT AND SAID WHAT OTHERS WERE THINKING:

I want to *knock his teeth out.*

What is it about that guy?

His money, mostly.

All the attack ads. They don't think he's earned it.

And the guy's just a *phony*.

They all make asses out of themselves sometimes.

Romney just takes it to another level.

WHO WANTS A DOUGH-NUT..?

Vote for me and you'll get one of THESE!

EIGHT YEARS AFTER HIS BRUTAL DEFEAT THERE, MCCAIN TOOK SOUTH CAROLINA.

For the last 28 years the winner of the South Carolina primary has been the nominee of our party...

RUDY FINISHED BEHIND RON PAUL. FRED THOMPSON FINISHED THIRD. MCCAIN AND MITT WERE HEADED FOR ONE LAST SHOWDOWN BEFORE SUPER TUESDAY: THIS TIME IN FLORIDA.

HUCKABEE STRUCK OUT IN A HIGHLY RELIGIOUS STATE.

There is no way to know at this point whether McCain or Romney will win.

FOX NEWS Channel · FRED BARNES

EVEN THOUGH HILLARY HAD REBOUNDED IN NEW HAMPSHIRE, SHE WAS ON THE DEFENSIVE. **THE SHIFT OF BLACK VOTERS MADE SOUTH CAROLINA LOOK LIKE A LOST CAUSE.**

HER CAMPAIGN SAID SHE WOULD SKIP THE STATE TO FOCUS ON THE JANUARY 19 NEVADA CAUCUSES INSTEAD.

He was a part-time state senator for a few years, and then he came to the Senate and immediately started running for president.

LOADED COMMENTS HAD A MOST SUSPICIOUS **WAY OF SLIPPING** OUT OF THE CLINTON CAMP.

SOMETIMES, THE MEDIA DID THE CLINTONS' WORK FOR THEM.

ON JANUARY 15 MICHIGAN HELD A PRIMARY THAT EVERYONE AGREED WAS MEANINGLESS.

ALONG WITH FLORIDA, MICHIGAN HAD MOVED UP ITS PRIMARY DATE IN DEFIANCE OF THE DEMOCRATIC PARTY'S OFFICIAL SCHEDULE.

THE PARTY TOLD MICHIGAN AND FLORIDA THEIR VOTES WOULDN'T COUNT. THE CANDIDATES PLEDGED NOT TO CAMPAIGN IN EITHER STATE.

MOST CANDIDATES, INCLUDING OBAMA, TOOK THEIR NAMES OFF THE MICHIGAN BALLOT. CLINTON STAYED ON. "IT'S CLEAR THIS ELECTION THEY'RE HAVING IS NOT GOING TO COUNT FOR ANYTHING."

EVEN SO, IT WAS A BAD SIGN THAT HILLARY ONLY PULLED 55 PERCENT OF THE VOTE IN THE STATE.

It's never good when 40 percent of the voters pass you over for "uncommitted."

WITH HER REPUTATION FOR NASTY TACTICS GROWING, HILLARY TRIED TO SCHMOOZE HER PRESS CORPS.

Welcome aboard the maiden flight of Hil Force One.

In the event of an unexpected drop in poll numbers, this plane will be diverted to New Hampshire.

FAA regulations prohibit the use of any cell phones, BlackBerries, or wireless devices that may be used to transmit a negative story about me.

Oy.

PRIVATELY, SHE WAS FUMING TOO.
CHARGES OF RACISM WERE OVERHYPED, THE CLINTONS FELT.

IS AMERICA READY FOR THIS NUTCRACKER?

STAINLESS STEEL THIGHS!

CRACKS TOUGHEST NUTS!

She scares me. I cross my legs every time she talks... *every time.*

[T]he reason she's a U.S. senator, the reason she's a candidate for president...

...the reason she may be a front-runner is *her husband messed around.*

WHILE SEXISM

COULD
BE FOUND

EVERY-WHERE.

STILL, HILLARY DIDN'T HAVE TO PUT UP WITH ANYTHING LIKE THE MYSTERIOUS CALLS SOME VOTERS REPORTED ON NEVADA CAUCUS DAY.

You just can't *take a chance* on Barack HUSSEIN Obama.

HILLARY STAYED ALIVE WITH A 51-45 WIN.

*FORESHADOWING

I hope the old saying "what happens in Vegas stays in Vegas" turns out to be true.*

JOHN EDWARDS? HE REGISTERED 4 PERCENT.

THAT SAME DAY, RICH CHICAGO BUSINESSMAN AND OBAMA FRIEND TONY REZKO WAS INDICTED FOR FRAUD AND EXTORTION.

When are you guys going to look into this Rezko stuff?

IT STINKS!

THE CLINTON CAMP DESPERATELY PUSHED THE STORY. BUT THE PRESS NEVER SAW A SMOKING GUN.

BUT THE BIGGER TEST, SOUTH CAROLINA, CAME A FEW DAYS LATER.

It's important that people are not just willing to say anything to get elected.

You gave a great speech in 2002 opposing the war in Iraq. By the next year the speech was off your Web site.

By the next year, you were telling reporters that you agreed with President Bush in his conduct of the war.

And by the next year, when you were in the Senate, you were voting to fund the war time after time after time.

AND ON JANUARY 21, A PRE-PRIMARY DEBATE TURNED UGLY.

I was fighting against [Republican] ideas —

— when you were practicing law and *representing your contributor, Rezko* —

— in his *slum landlord business* in inner-city Chicago!

THAT BITTERNESS SPILLED BACK ONTO THE TRAIL. BILL REMAINED CONVINCED THE MEDIA WAS OUT TO GET HILLARY.

THIS ANGRY NEW BILL CLINTON WAS BAFFLING.

OBAMA EVEN SAID IN ONE DEBATE, "I CAN'T TELL WHO I'M RUNNING AGAINST SOMETIMES."

HE TOLD INTERVIEWERS BILL HAD GONE TOO FAR.

BUT IT WASN'T UNTIL PRIMARY DAY THAT ONE UNFORGETTABLE, CHURLISH COMMENT DESTROYED BILL'S REPUTATION IN BLACK AMERICA.

Jesse Jackson won South Carolina twice, in '84 and '88. And he ran a good campaign. And Senator Obama's run a good campaign here, he's run a good campaign everywhere.*

*TRANSLATION: HE ONLY WON BECAUSE HE'S BLACK.

He didn't just cream her with the black vote — white voters, too.

Jesse Jackson didn't do that.

OBAMA CRUSHED HILLARY IN SOUTH CAROLINA BY A STUNNING 55-26 MARGIN.

OBAMA'S MOJO WAS BACK.

CHANGE WE CAN BELIEVE IN

AND THEN CAME A STUNNING BLOW TO HILLARY.

And in Barack Obama, I see not just the audacity, but the possibility of hope for the America that is yet to be....

What counts in our leadership is not the length of years in Washington, but the reach of our vision, the strength of our beliefs... It is time for a new generation of leadership.

So it is with Barack Obama. It is time again for a new generation of leadership. It is time now for Barack Obama.

OBAM

And lo, the torch was passed...

He blind-sided us...

ON THE REPUBLICAN SIDE, SOUTH CAROLINA HAD WINNOWED THE FIELD.

DUNCAN HUNTER WAS OUT, WITH A GRAND TOTAL OF ONE DELEGATE. (WHO EVEN KNEW HE WAS STILL RUNNING?)

AND FOR FRED THOMPSON, WHO ONCE SAID SOUTH CAROLINA WOULD BE HIS "FIREWALL," **IT WAS TIME TO ADMIT THE OBVIOUS.**

He quit... by *press release?!*

THAT MADE IT MORE OF A ROMNEY-MCCAIN RACE THAN EVER.

IN THE FLORIDA SAND THE FINAL BATTLE LINES WERE DRAWN.

It's important to have a president who's had a real job.

One of my opponents wanted to set a date for withdrawal that would have meant *disaster....*

If we *surrender* and wave a white flag, like Senator Clinton wants to do, and withdraw, as Governor Romney wanted to do...

...then there will be chaos, genocide, and the cost of American blood and treasure would be dramatically higher.

FOR MITT: THE ECONOMY

FOR MCCAIN: THE WAR

MCCAIN WAS DREDGING UP **A YEAR-OLD COMMENT BY ROMNEY.**

There's no question that the president and Prime Minister al-Maliki have to have a series of timetables and milestones that they speak about.

But those shouldn't be for public pronouncement. You don't want the enemy to understand how long they have to wait in the weeds until you're going to be gone.

That's what McCain means by "date for withdrawal"?

I didn't think McCain played like that.

Ah, they're all the fucking same.

Anyway, Romney deserves it. He was blowing in the wind like usual.

MITT FOUGHT BACK:

That's simply wrong and it's dishonest, and he should apologize....

He's trying desperately to change the topic from the economy and trying to get back to Iraq.

BUT MCCAIN DIDN'T BACK DOWN.

The apology is owed to the young men and women serving this nation in uniform....

He said that he wanted a timetable for withdrawal – that would have meant disaster.

That would have meant that Al-Qaeda would now be telling the world that they defeated the United States of America.

THE FINAL DAYS OF THE FLORIDA CAMPAIGN WERE A VICIOUS BLUR.

Hi, I'm calling on behalf of Mitt Romney. John McCain and Ted Kennedy wrote an *amnesty* bill.

And McCain teamed with another *liberal Democrat* to write campaign finance reform. John McCain also joined with Democrats to vote against the Bush tax cuts....

No wonder former Senate Republican leader Rick Santorum said, quote, "John McCain was not only against us, but leading the charge on the other side."

IN THE END, IT WAS BETTER TO BE A HERO THAN A BUSINESSMAN.

sigh

Florida polling results have been called:
McCain: 36
Romney: 31

RUDY FINISHED A DISTANT THIRD. IT WAS THE END OF THE ROAD FOR THE FORMER FRONT-RUNNER. HE WAS OUT THE NEXT DAY.

I am very proud to endorse my friend... a hero....

Heh. That's all about hating Mitt.

WITH 21 STATES SET TO VOTE ON SUPER TUESDAY, **POLLS SHOWED MCCAIN IN COMMAND.**

CONSERVATIVES WERE PANICKING.

> John McCain has done more to *hurt the Republican Party* than any elected official I know of.

> If he's our candidate, then Hillary's going to be our girl. She's more conservative than he is. *I will campaign for her* if it's McCain.

ROMNEY JUST COULDN'T REBOUND FROM LOSING FLORIDA. FEBRUARY 5 WAS MCCAIN'S CORONATION.

CONSERVATIVE MCCAIN HATERS (AND THERE WERE PLENTY) **WANTED HIM TO HANG ON,**

BUT THE NEXT DAY... ROMNEY FACED UP TO REALITY.

> If I fight on in my campaign, all the way to the convention, I would forestall the launch of a national campaign and make it more likely that Senator Clinton or Obama would win.

> And in this time of war, I simply cannot let my campaign, be a part of aiding a surrender to terror....

> I feel that I now have to stand aside for my party and my country.

OBAMA WAS SOARING.
SOON AFTER THE KENNEDY ENDORSEMENT,
HE ANNOUNCED $38 MILLION
RAISED IN JANUARY — MORE THAN A MILLION PER DAY.

OUTFUNDED AND LOSING MOMENTUM, HILLARY WAS GETTING DESPERATE. ON JANUARY 29, SHE FLEW TO FLORIDA FOR THE STATE'S MEANINGLESS PRIMARY.

HILLARY BEAT OBAMA THERE ON THE STRENGTH OF HER NAME RECOGNITION.

AND EVEN THOUGH NEITHER CANDIDATE HAD CAMPAIGNED, SHE TREATED IT LIKE A REAL VICTORY. **PEOPLE DIDN'T BUY IT.** BUT CLINTON AIDES PRESSED THEIR CASE.

JOHN EDWARDS, MEANWHILE, FINALLY GAVE UP HIS FIGHT.

BUT HE'D SOON BE BACK, IN ANOTHER CONTEXT...

RICHARDSON
WAS OUT, TOO.
AND KUCINICH.
AND GRAVEL.
(NOT THAT ANYONE NOTICED.)

YOU NEVER KNOW WHEN YOU'RE GOING TO MEET A **BLACK ELVIS ON THE TRAIL.**

IT WAS BECOMING A FULL-BLOWN CULTURAL PHENOMENON.

BUT WHILE THE CLINTONITES SNEERED AT THE HYPE, THE CROWDS WERE REAL — EVEN IN A RED STATE LIKE IDAHO.

SUPER TUESDAY

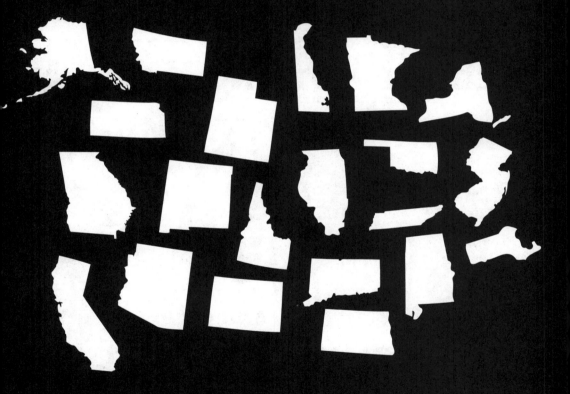

AT LAST CAME FEBRUARY 5:
SUPER TUESDAY.
22 PRIMARIES FROM COAST TO COAST.

Key Assumption: 5 February likely to decide nominee.

HAROLD ICKES

THE CLINTON CAMPAIGN HAD HOPED TO THROW A KNOCKOUT PUNCH.

BUT THE NATIONAL PRIMARY THAT WAS SUPPOSED TO DECIDE THE RACE DECIDED NOTHING.

AND ON FEBRUARY 6, AMERICA WOKE UP TO A DEADLOCK.

EVERY SPIN HAD A COUNTER-SPIN.

Obama won more states.

Hillary won bigger states.

She should've won Missouri.

Obama should've won Massachusetts.

WHICH LEFT HILLARY WITH A NEW PROBLEM:

What do you mean "we're out of money"?

THE CLINTONS WEREN'T POOR.
THEY'D RAKED IN OVER $100 MILLION SINCE LEAVING THE WHITE HOUSE.
SHE PUT $6 MILLION OF IT INTO HER CAMPAIGN.
BUT IT WAS STARTING TO LOOK LIKE TOO LITTLE, TOO LATE.

**FEBRUARY WAS A DISASTER FOR HILLARY.
SHE LOST 10 STATES IN A ROW TO OBAMA —
MOSTLY IN PLACES SHE DIDN'T EVEN CONTEST.**

HER TEAM HAD EXPECTED THE RACE TO BE OVER BY FEBRUARY 5.

FOR THAT MISCALCULATION, HER LONGTIME CONFIDANTE AND CAMPAIGN MANAGER, PATTI SOLIS DOYLE, WAS THROWN OVERBOARD.

WITH THE MEDIA SWOONING FOR OBAMA...

The feeling most people get when they hear Barack Obama's speech--

I felt this *thrill going up my leg*.

...CLINTON'S GROWING FRUSTRATION WAS OBVIOUS.

THERE WAS THE **FLAILING CHARGE** THAT OBAMA WAS LIFTING FROM **ANOTHER** POLITICIAN'S SPEECHES.

AT ONE EVENT, HER ANGER AT A MISLEADING **OBAMA** MAILER ABOUT HER POLICIES BOILED OVER.

If your candidacy is going to be about words then they should be *your own words*.

Lifting whole passages from someone else's speeches is not change you can believe in, it's *change you can Xerox*.

Now I could stand up here and say, let's get everybody together, let's get unified.

The sky will open, the light will come down, *celestial choirs* will be singing.

And everyone will know we should do the right thing, and the *world will be perfect*.

But I have no illusions about how hard this is going to be. You are not going to *wave a magic wand* and make the special interests disappear.

I think she might be losing it.

She's got a point.

Senator Obama, are you *comfortable?* Can we *get you* anything?

SOME OF THAT MOCKERY WAS CATCHING ON, ACTUALLY. *SATURDAY NIGHT LIVE* SPOOFED THE MEDIA FOR KISSING UP TO HIM.

SNL EVEN SEEMED TO EMBARRASS THE PRESS **INTO TOUGHER** COVERAGE OF OBAMA.

BUT THEN HILLARY TOOK A DECIDEDLY **SERIOUS TURN.**

POTUS

3:00 AM

THINGS WERE TENSE ALL RIGHT.

OBAMA SUPPORTERS WERE QUICK TO REMIND PEOPLE OF RECENT HISTORY.

Now, one of Clinton's laws of politics is this. If one candidate is trying to scare you and the other one's trying to get you to think...

...if one candidate is appealing to your fears and the other one is appealing to your hopes, you better vote for the person who wants you to think and hope.

A "SNUB" AT THE STATE OF THE UNION BECAME A TWO-DAY STORY.

I think he was wrong to turn away... because if you are triumphant you don't have to stand on the person's throat.

IT EVEN MADE *THE VIEW.*

OBAMA FINISHED FEBRUARY WITH 10 STRAIGHT WINS. HILLARY HAD LOST HER OVERALL LEAD IN DELEGATES.

OBAMA WAS NOW
★ OFFICIALLY ★
THE FRONT-RUNNER.

BUT CLINTON STILL HAD AN EDGE IN "SUPERDELEGATES" — PARTY INSIDERS WHO GET A VOTE, IN PART AS A CHECK AGAINST THE PRIMARY VOTERS. SOME PEOPLE CALLED IT UNDEMOCRATIC. IN THEORY, THE UNDECIDED SUPERDELEGATES COULD GET TOGETHER AND HAND IT TO HILLARY.

BUT NOW EVEN SOME OF THOSE INSIDERS WHO HAD BEEN WITH HILLARY WERE HAVING **SECOND**

THOUGHTS.

> Something is happening in America, and people are prepared and ready to make that great leap.

SOMETHING CERTAINLY WAS HAPPENING. WHILE HILLARY HAD GONE BROKE, OBAMA WAS SHATTERING RECORDS.

> I just got off the phone with Chicago. Obama's going to announce $55 million raised.

> *This year?*

> *This month!!*

TEXAS
MARCH 4

If she wins in Texas and Ohio, I think she'll be the nominee.

If you don't deliver for her, I don't think she can be.

THE MARCH 4 PRIMARIES IN TEXAS AND OHIO GAVE HILLARY A CHANCE TO BREAK **OBAMA'S MOMENTUM.** SHE LED IN BOTH STATES, BUT BY A NARROWING MARGIN.

BILL WAS TELLING VOTERS **THEY HAD TO KEEP HILLARY ALIVE.**

HILLARY WAS COMING TO REALIZE THAT HER "BASE" WAS WOMEN AND WORKING-CLASS WHITE VOTERS, PEOPLE WITH ECONOMIC ANXIETY. SHE AIRED AN AD SHOWING HERSELF **WORKING THE "NIGHT SHIFT."**

I don't think people should come to Ohio and tell the people of Ohio one thing —

— and then have your campaign tell a foreign government something else behind closed doors.

A LEAKED MEMO SUGGESTED THAT A TOP OBAMA ADVISOR TOLD THE CANADIAN GOVERNMENT THAT HIS ANTI-NAFTA RHETORIC WAS "POLITICAL POSITIONING."

HILLARY GAINED GROUND IN TEXAS AND OHIO... BUT NOT ENOUGH.

For everyone who has been... counted out and refused to be knocked out...

...who works hard and never gives up, this one is for you...

...this nation's coming back and so is this campaign.

THE MEDIA FOCUSED ON HILLARY'S BIG WINS. BUT THE NOMINATION IS ABOUT DELEGATES, **NOT WINS AND LOSSES.**

AND BACK AT OBAMA'S CHICAGO HEADQUARTERS, **HIS STAFF WAS FOCUSED ON THE ALL-IMPORTANT DELEGATE COUNT.**

THEY HAD THE LEAD, AND THEIR PROJECTIONS WERE FOR IT TO GROW.

MEANWHILE BACK AT CLINTON HEADQUARTERS, THE SAME REALIZATION WAS DAWNING, WITH A SENSE OF DREAD — AND RECRIMINATIONS.

EXPLETIVE *YOU!!*

EXPLETIVE *YOU!!*

EXPLETIVE *YOU!!*

JUST THEN, IN A DIFFERENT ROOM:

PHIL SINGER, THE CAMPAIGN'S DEPUTY COMMUNICATIONS DIRECTOR, EMERGED FROM A MEETING ON FEB. 11 AND WITHOUT EXPLANATION STARTED ANGRILY CURSING THE WAR ROOM.

EXPLETIVE *ALL OF YOU!!*

AR ROOM

ACCORDING TO A WITNESS, HE SHOUTED AND STORMED OUT AND DID NOT RETURN FOR SEVERAL DAYS.

CLINTON HAD THROWN HER CAMPAIGN MANAGER OVERBOARD.

BUT HER ARROGANT **AND SOCIALLY** AWKWARD POLLSTER, **MARK PENN, HAD BECOME THE REAL VILLAIN.**

She is a monster, too— *that is off the record—*

—she is stooping to anything.

EVERYONE SEEMED TO BE LOSING THEIR COOL—INCLUDING OBAMA'S FOREIGN POLICY ADVISOR, SAMANTHA POWER.

Jeez, these days, *nothing* is off the record.

Pfft. That's not how we used to do it. There's no *honor* left in this game.

GERALDINE FERRARO

If Obama was *a white man*, he would not be in this position. He happens to be very lucky to be who he is.

HA!

This is an *epic time* to be a white guy *with a master's...*

WITH THE NOMINATION **SLIPPING AWAY**, **THE CLINTON TEAM** TRIED TO CHANGE THE RULES, PUSHING HARD TO COUNT **THE MICHIGAN AND FLORIDA PRIMARIES** — OR AT LEAST HOLD RE-VOTES.

BUT THE ODDS OF **EXPENSIVE AND CONTROVERSIAL DO-OVERS WERE LOOKING SLIM.**

THE DOOR SEEMED TO BE CLOSING FOR HILLARY.

BUT THEN...
AN EXPLOSIVE VIDEOTAPE SURFACED.

FOR OBAMA, THIS WAS NOT THE PATH TO VICTORY IN HEAVILY WORKING-CLASS PENNSYLVANIA.

THE MEDIA WAS IN A FRENZY.
OBAMA HAD TO DO SOMETHING.

He contains within him the *contradictions* — the good and the bad — of the community that he has served diligently for so many years.

I can no more disown him than I can disown the black community. I can no more disown him than I can my white grandmother.

Beautiful. And *he wrote it himself.*

Yeah, but how will it play in the Rust Belt?

MANY CLINTONITES BELIEVED AMERICA WOULDN'T ELECT A BLACK MAN — ESPECIALLY ONE WHO'D NEVER FACED THE REPUBLICAN ATTACK MACHINE BEFORE.

wulla wulla walla walla walla wulla walla wulla walla walla wulla wulla walla wulla walla wulla walla walla wulla walla walla wu

TO THEM, JEREMIAH WRIGHT
WAS PROOF OF IT.

THERE WAS ONE SUPERDELEGATE THE CLINTONS WERE DESPERATE NOT TO LOSE — A MAN CLINTON HAD NAMED TO HIS CABINET.

NO DICE.

JAMES CARVILLE

Judas.

ONE SIGN THAT OBAMA WAS PULLING AWAY:

JOHN McCAIN WAS STARTING TO TARGET *HIM.*

> Senator Obama said that if Al-Qaeda came back to Iraq after American troops are withdrawn, then he would send military troops back.

> I have some news: Al-Qaeda *is* in Iraq. I will not surrender. I *will not surrender* to Al-Qaeda.

OBAMA'S WIFE, MICHELLE, GAVE HIM AN EASY OPENING.

> For the first time in my adult life, I'm really proud of my country...

> ...because it feels like hope is making a comeback.

SHE DIDN'T QUITE MEAN IT THAT WAY. BUT IN A PATTERN THAT WOULD ENDURE, THE McCAIN TEAM POUNCED ON ANY CHANCE TO QUESTION OBAMA'S PATRIOTISM.

> I AM proud of my country. I don't know about you...

> I just wanted to make the statement that I have been and always will be proud of my country.

AS HE WAITED FOR A DEMOCRATIC NOMINEE TO EMERGE, McCAIN HAD THE LUXURY OF RELAXING...

AND MAKING NICE WITH HIS FRIENDS IN THE PRESS CORPS.

BUT THE MEDIA'S RULES OF COVERING McCAIN WERE BEGINNING TO CHANGE.

For McCain, Self-Confidence on Ethics Poses Its Own Risk

As his relationship with a female lobbyist underscores, John McCain's confidence in his own integrity sometimes seems to blind him to potential conflicts.

Readers shared their thoughts on this article.

MCCAIN FURIOUSLY DENIED HAVING AN AFFAIR WITH VICKI ISEMAN — AND WENT AFTER *THE TIMES.*

> Are these the standards of the *New York Times?*

> No. They are the standards of the *National Enquirer.*

Dear McCain Supporter,

Well, here we go. We could expect attacks were coming; as soon as John McCain appeared to be locking up the Republican nomination, the liberal establishment and their allies at the New York Times have gone on the attack. Today's front-page New York Times story is particularly disgusting — an un-sourced hit-and-run smear campaign designed to distract from the issues at stake in this election. With John McCain leading a number o[f]

THE STORM PASSED. NO ONE COULD PROVE AN AFFAIR.

AND, WITH WINS IN TEXAS AND OHIO, MCCAIN FINALLY CLINCHED THE NOMINATION.

> Senator McCain, given President Bush's low approval ratings, will this be a negative or a positive for you? And how much do you hope he'll campaign for you on the trail?

> REC

> I hope that he will campaign for me as much as is keeping with his *busy schedule.*

A VISIT WITH BUSH — HOWEVER AWKWARD — MADE IT OFFICIAL.

The New York Times

THURSDAY, MARCH 4, 2008

BUSH APPROVAL FALLS TO 30 PERCEN[T]

(THAT SCHEDULE TURNED OUT TO BE PRETTY "BUSY.")

IN LATE MARCH, HILLARY WAS PUSHING THE "EXPERIENCE" LINE AGAIN.
THIS TIME, SHE PUSHED IT TOO FAR.

IT REMINDED PEOPLE...

...THAT YOU CAN'T ALWAYS TRUST THE CLINTONS.

HILLARY SHOULD DROP OUT.

BUT THE MORE SHE WAS PRESSURED **TO GET OUT,** THE MORE HILLARY AND HER SUPPORTERS **DUG IN.**

HILLARY'S TOP STRATEGIST, MARK PENN, WAS BECOMING FAMOUS FOR HIS COMICALLY *STRAINED SPIN.*

Could we possibly have a nominee who hasn't won any of the *significant states* -- outside of Illinois? That raises some serious questions about Sen. Obama.

"Significant states"?

Winning Democratic primaries is not a qualification or a sign of who can win the general election.

HE ALSO RAN A HUGE WASHINGTON PR FIRM WITH SOME UNSAVORY CLIENTS. HE WAS AN EASY TARGET.

BUT THE CLINTONS **TRUSTED HIM** TOO MUCH TO DUMP HIM. HE WAS THEIR GURU.

Senator Obama really can't win the general election.

BUT WORD THAT HE'D MET WITH THE COLOMBIAN GOVERNMENT TO HELP THEM LOBBY FOR A FREE TRADE DEAL THAT HILLARY OPPOSED WAS **JUST TOO MUCH.**

SHE HAD TO PROTECT HER NEW FIGHTING POPULIST IMAGE:

SHE WAS THE **"FIGHTER"** WHO REFUSED TO QUIT.

Jace, it's Harlan; *Penn's out.*

Good Riddance!

MEANWHILE, OBAMA'S CRITICS MOCKED HIM AS AN "ELITIST."

You go into some of these small towns in Pennsylvania, and like a lot of small towns in the Midwest, the jobs have been gone now for 25 years and nothing's replaced them....

And it's not surprising then they get bitter, they cling to guns or religion or antipathy to people who aren't like them or anti-immigrant sentiment or anti-trade sentiment as a way to explain their frustrations.

AT A CLOSED-DOOR SAN FRANCISCO FUND-RAISER, OBAMA WAS RECORDED — UNBEKNOWNST TO HIM — **BY A HUFFINGTON POST BLOGGER.**

TO PROVE WHICH CANDIDATE WAS MORE "AUTHENTIC,"
MORE IN TOUCH WITH THE STATE'S VOTERS.

OR... WHITE ENOUGH.

BUT HILLARY WAS STILL IN DEEP TROUBLE. SHE'D WON THE STATE — BUT THANKS TO THE PARTY'S COMPLEX DELEGATE RULES, SHE GAINED LITTLE GROUND ON OBAMA.

If Senator Obama can't win a big state like Pennsylvania with that enormous spending advantage...

...just what will it take for him to win a large swing state?

HER CAMPAIGN INSISTED WINNING BIG STATES WAS MORE IMPORTANT THAN WINNING DELEGATES.

THE CLINTON TEAM LOVED TO SEE OBAMA'S OLD FRIEND AND PASTOR KEEP POPPING BACK UP:

Louis Farrakhan is one of the most important voices in the 20th and 21st century. Louis Farrakhan is not my enemy. He did not put me in chains, he did not put me in slavery, and he didn't make me this color...

This most recent attack on the black church is not an attack on Jeremiah Wright; it is an attack on the black church.

I am outraged by the comments that were made and saddened over the spectacle that we saw yesterday. I've known Reverend Wright for almost 20 years. The person that I saw yesterday was not the person that I met 20 years ago.

His comments were not only *divisive* and *destructive*, but I believe that they end up giving comfort to *those who prey on hate.*

DESPITE WHAT OBAMA HAD SAID, IT WAS TIME FOR SOME DISOWNING.

WITH JUST A HANDFUL OF VOTES LEFT, THE PRIMARY CALENDAR WAS FINALLY WINDING DOWN.

"AREA MAN PUMPING *HIS OWN* GASOLINE."

EVEN HILLARY SUPPORTERS AGREED THAT TWO MAY 6 PRIMARIES WOULD BE HER LAST GASP.

The people in the press who haven't been particularly on our side anyway...

They say, *"Poor ol' Bill Clinton has been sent out to the country."*

Like I've been *banished.*

WHILE BILL STUMPED FURIOUSLY IN RURAL NORTH CAROLINA, PLAYING THE POPULIST CARD TO THE HILT.

HILLARY WON INDIANA — BARELY BY ONE POINT. BUT NORTH CAROLINA WAS A BLOWOUT.

OBAMA CRUSHED HER BY 15 POINTS, NEARLY WIPING OUT HER DELEGATE GAINS IN PENNSYLVANIA.

IT WAS TIME TO SAY THE OBVIOUS:

We now know who the Democratic nominee's going to be... and *no one's going to dispute it.*

NEW YORK POST
LATE CITY FINAL
2 CE

Hil blows last shot in Indy ...aler, ...feat

TOAST!

OR MAYBE IT WASN'T SO OBVIOUS.

I have a much broader base to build a winning coalition on.

Senator Obama's support among working, hardworking Americans, *white Americans,* is weakening again.

HILLARY JUST WOULDN'T QUIT. **SHE OFFERED SOME STRANGE RATIONALES.**

WHITE Americans? WTF??

She's lost me for good.

IN EARLY MAY OBAMA WAS LEADING EVEN AMONG SUPERDELEGATES. *THE MATH WAS CLEAR:* HILLARY HAD ALMOST NO WAY TO WIN. **BUT SHE SOLDIERED ON.**

I just don't wanna vote for a – I'm not racist or anything...

...but I just don't want somebody *in there like that.*

CRITICS NOTED THAT SHE DREW SUPPORT FROM SOME UNPALATABLE QUARTERS. IN THE APPALACHIAN STATES OF KENTUCKY AND WEST VIRGINIA, HILLARY WON IN BLOWOUTS.

SOME PEOPLE EVEN ACCUSED HER OF THE DARKEST THOUGHTS.

Why don't you drop out?

My husband did not wrap up the nomination in 1992 until he won the California primary somewhere in the middle of June, right?

We all remember Bobby Kennedy was assassinated in June in California. You know I just, I don't understand it.

IT WAS CLEAR, THOUGH, THAT NOTHING WAS GOING TO STOP OBAMA. IN PORTLAND, OREGON, 75,000 PEOPLE SHOWED UP TO SEE HIM.

DESPERATE, HILLARY FLEW TO FLORIDA HOPING TO MAKE ITS VOTES COUNT.

The lesson of 2000 here in Florida is crystal clear: if any votes aren't counted, the will of the people isn't realized and our democracy is diminished.

We're seeing that right now in Zimbabwe. Tragically, an election was held, the president lost, they refused to abide by the will of the people.

Zimbabwe??

DEMOCRATIC PARTY OFFICIALS DISAGREED, GIVING FLORIDA AND MICHIGAN DELEGATES ONLY HALF-VOTES.

HILLARY'S LAST HOPE AT AN UPSET WAS GONE. HER SUPPORTERS WERE FURIOUS.

IT WAS ALL OVER BUT THE SHOUTING. THE LAST PRIMARIES CAME ON JUNE 3. OBAMA WON IN MONTANA AND ROLLED OUT 60 SUPERDELEGATE ENDORSEMENTS, ENOUGH TO BREAK THE "MAGIC NUMBER" OF 2,117 AND LOCK UP THE NOMINATION.

> Tonight I can stand here and say that *I will be the Democratic nominee for president of the United States of America.*

> Even when the pundits and the naysayers proclaimed week after week that this race was over, you kept on voting...

> Now, the question is: Where do we go from here? And given how far we've come and where we need to go as a party, it's a question I don't take lightly. This has been a long campaign, and I will be making no decisions tonight.

FOR A MOMENT, IT SEEMED AS THOUGH HILLARY MIGHT ACTUALLY FIGHT ON TO THE CONVENTION IN DENVER. SHE DIDN'T DROP OUT, OR ENDORSE.

BUT ONLY FOR A MOMENT. FOUR DAYS LATER, THE CLINTON FOR PRESIDENT CAMPAIGN WAS HISTORY.

> Today, as I suspend my campaign, I congratulate him on the victory he has won and the extraordinary race he has run. I endorse him and throw my full support behind him.

> And I ask all of you to join me in working as hard for Barack Obama as you have for me.

> Although we weren't able to shatter that highest, hardest glass ceiling this time, thanks to you, it's got about 18 million cracks in it.

> And the light is shining through like never before, filling us all with the hope and the sure knowledge that the path will be a little easier next time.

AS THE DEMOCRATS WRAPPED THINGS UP, THINGS WERE NOT GOING WELL FOR McCAIN.

THE MEDIA WAS ALL OVER THE LOBBYISTS WHO WERE RUNNING THE CAMPAIGN OF A MAN WHO'D MADE A CAREER OUT OF ATTACKING LOBBYISTS.

ON THE NIGHT OBAMA CLAIMED THE NOMINATION, McCAIN TRIED TO FRAME THE RACE WITH HIS OWN BIG SPEECH.

That's not change —

— we can believe in.

IT WAS A DISASTER — WIDELY PANNED EVEN BY CONSERVATIVES ON FOX NEWS.

I don't think it was a successful speech. I think he came off as just sniping at Senator Obama.

BILL KRISTOL

THE SPEECH ALSO CONTAINED ONE OF THE FUNNIEST MALAPROPISMS OF THE CAMPAIGN:

We should be able to deliver *bottled hot water* to dehydrated babies and rescue the infirm from a hospital with no electricity.

When Americans confront a catastrophe they have a right to expect basic competence from their government.

This blogger *Atrios* says the green background made McCain look "like the *cottage cheese in a lime jello salad...* Awesome in how dreadful it was."

Wait... *hot water bottles?*

AND THE MISCUES KEPT COMING...

It's common knowledge that Al-Qaeda is going back into Iran and receiving training and coming back into Iraq from Iran.

That's well known. And it's unfortunate.

I'm sorry, the *Iranians* are training extremists, not Al-Qaeda.

FOR THE MOMENT, AT LEAST, THINGS WERE LOOKING GOOD FOR OBAMA.

Maybe it's instinct, but I keep waiting for that other shoe to drop...

OBAMA VS MCCAIN

WITH HILLARY OUT, IT WAS RECONCILIATION TIME.

STEP ONE:
A SECRET PRIVATE MEETING
IN WASHINGTON.

She rocks.

She rocks. That's the point I'm trying to make.

AND, SOON AFTER, A MORE PUBLIC DISPLAY...
IN A TOWN CALLED *UNITY,* **NO LESS.**

I don't even think it's a close call. How do you not pick Hillary Clinton?

We would sweep all across the country. It would be a bold move: first African American, first woman. History!

TERRY MCAULIFFE

A DEBATE RAGED ABOUT A POSSIBLE JOINT TICKET.

Obama's first imperative is... a clear assertion of his absolute right to choose his own running mate...

and not be pressured into a decision by the Clintons or their friends.

DAVID BRODER

BEHIND THE SCENES, RESENTMENT FESTERED. BILL SEETHED OVER **HIS DAMAGED REPUTATION.**

I am not a racist, I never made a racist comment, and I did not attack him personally...

BILL RICHARDSON!

THE CLINTONS EVEN KEPT AN "ENEMIES LIST" OF THOSE WHO'D BETRAYED THEM.

THEIR SUPPORTERS DIDN'T SEEM READY TO FORGIVE EITHER.

P.U.M.A.

BUT FIRST A MOMENT OF SILENCE, TAKEN FOR THOSE TAKEN FROM US...

TIM RUSSERT
MAY 7, 1950 – JUNE 13, 2008

Godspeed, Tim, my boy... wherever you are.

I'm sure you'll make the rest of us all look lazy from Heaven too.

WITH HILLARY ON HIS SIDE, OBAMA MOVED INTO GENERAL ELECTION MODE. THAT MEANT TRIMMING HIS SAILS ON A FEW TRICKY ISSUES.

IT SEEMED SOME OF THE OBAMA GLOW WAS WEARING OFF.

You're *allowed* to laugh at him!!

OR COULD YOU?

A SATIRICAL *NEW YORKER* COVER STIRRED OUTRAGE ON THE LEFT.

OCCASIONALLY, THOUGH, OBAMA MADE IT EASY:

LIKE WHEN HIS CAMPAIGN ROLLED OUT A NEW LOGO.

AND WAS HE MAYBE GETTING A LITTLE TOO CLOSE TO CELEBRITY WORLD?

How can he return these *personal* e-mails? But *he does!*

SCARLETT JOHANSSON

COME JULY, MCCAIN WAS STUCK IN THE DOLDRUMS.

LAGGING IN THE POLLS, LACKING A CLEAR MESSAGE. IT WAS TIME FOR ANOTHER CAMPAIGN SHAKEUP.

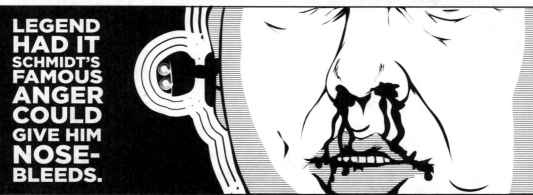

LEGEND HAD IT SCHMIDT'S **FAMOUS ANGER COULD** GIVE HIM **NOSE- BLEEDS.**

DETERMINED TO SHOW HE COULD BE A WORLD LEADER, OBAMA TOOK HIS FIRST MAJOR **OVERSEAS TRIP.**

HE STARTED WITH A VISIT TO TROOPS IN AFGHANISTAN.

IT WAS A **SWISH** WITH THE **MEDIA.**

AND THEN TO IRAQ, WHERE THE PRIME MINISTER SAID HE AGREED WITH OBAMA'S VISION OF WITHDRAWING U.S. TROOPS QUICKLY.

BACK IN AMERICA, MCCAIN TRASHED OBAMA FOR OPPOSING THE "SURGE," WHICH HAD HELPED TO STABILIZE THE COUNTRY.

We *rejected* the audacity of *hopelessness*...

...*and we were right.*

BUT MCCAIN WAS FINDING IT HARD TO COMPETE ON THE MEDIA STAGE.

GEN. DAVID PETRAEUS

ON A DAY WHEN OBAMA TOURED **IRAQ WITH A TOP GENERAL**...

...MCCAIN RODE IN A GOLF CART WITH THE **OCTOGENARIAN** FATHER OF A DEEPLY UNPOPULAR PRESIDENT.

THUS WROUGHT HIS APOTHEOSIS IN BERLIN:

Tonight, I speak to you not as a candidate for president, but as a citizen — a proud citizen of the United States, and a fellow citizen of the world.

I know my country has not perfected itself. We've made our share of mistakes, and there are times when our actions around the world have not lived up to our best intentions.

But I also know how much I love America.

OVERSEAS, OBAMA WAS A SMASH HIT.

DER SPIEGEL

Deutschland trifft der SuperStar!

Pricing USD$3.59 IN GERMANY
Pricing USD$3.59
Precio USD$3.59
Pricing USD$3.59
Pricing USD$3.59

9 780975 915202

BUT THE MCCAIN TEAM SAW OBAMA'S TRIP AS A CHANCE TO TURN HIS STRENGTH INTO A WEAKNESS:

CELEB RITY

BEHIND THE MOCKERY, OBAMA SAW A MORE SINISTER STRATEGY AT WORK:

What they're going to try to do is make you scared of me.

You know, *he doesn't look like all those other presidents on the dollar bills.*

Barack Obama has played *the race card,* and he played it from the *bottom of the deck.*

It's divisive, negative, shameful, and *wrong.*

RICK DAVIS

AND JUST WHEN THE WORLD HAD ALL BUT FORGOTTEN ABOUT JOHN EDWARDS...

BACK ON THE TRAIL, MCCAIN WAS LOOKING FOR VOTES WHEREVER HE COULD FIND THEM.

AND DEMOCRATS WERE GETTING *NERVOUS*.

BUT EVEN AS MCCAIN TRIED TO FOCUS ON A DANGEROUS WORLD...

We are all Georgians now.

...HE KEPT DOING OBAMA FAVORS.

Senator, how many houses do you own?

I think — I'll have my staff get to you...

It's condominiums where — I'll have them get to you.

THE CORRECT **ANSWER** WAS EIGHT.

I'm going to be honest: I know a lot less about economics than I do about military and foreign policy issues.

I still need to be educated.

FOR A RICH GUY, **MCCAIN** NEVER TOOK MUCH INTEREST IN ECONOMICS.

HIS CAMPAIGN **ADVISORS WEREN'T HELPING MUCH,** EITHER.

PHIL GRAMM

You've heard of mental depression; this is a mental recession.

We have sort of become a nation of *whiners.*

IN AUGUST, OBAMA FINALLY UNVEILED HIS RUNNING MATE – SENDING A SIGNAL ABOUT FOREIGN POLICY EXPERIENCE AND WORKING-CLASS ROOTS.

JOE BIDEN

I was an Irish-Catholic kid from Scranton. My dad always said, "Champ, it's not how many times you get knocked down, it's how quickly you get up..."

Ladies and gentlemen, that's your story. That's America's story.

SOME HILLARY SUPPORTERS WERE STILL BITTER: THEY HAD WANTED *HER* ON THE TICKET.

BUT ONCE THE DEMOCRATIC CONVENTION STARTED, DEMOCRATS WERE REMINDED OF WHAT BROUGHT THEM TOGETHER.

I pledge to you that I will be there next January on the floor of the United States Senate when we begin the great test.

THE DEMOCRATS FOUND PARTY UNITY.

No way. No how. No McCain!

Barack Obama is my candidate.

And he *must* be our president.

Barack Obama is ready to be president of the United States.

You sure his fingers weren't crossed?

Heh.

Wow... never thought he'd bring himself to say that.

Yo Harlan, are you guys on the list for the *Vanity Fair* party?

HUFFINGTON POST

Can you hook me up?

AS OBAMA GOT READY **TO ACCEPT THE** NOMINATION OUTDOORS AT DENVER'S INVESCO FIELD, REPUBLICANS WERE MOCKING HIM AGAIN.

A football stadium equipped with a movie set that looks like a Greek temple?

The polls are overestimating Obama, just as he is overestimating himself.

RUSH LIMBAUGH

BUT WHEN THE MOMENT CAME, THERE WAS NO MOCKERY,

ONLY HISTORY IN THE MAKING.

I accept your nomination for presidency of the United States.

SOME DEMOCRATS HADN'T FELT SO HAPPY IN YEARS.

BUT YOU CAN NEVER PREDICT POLIT

RUMORS
WERE FLYING.
BUT MOST OF THEM MISSED THE AMAZING
TRUTH.

HER 17-YEAR-OLD
DAUGHTER, BRISTOL,
WAS PREGNANT.

THE GOP CONVENTION KICKED OFF WITH
A FRENZY OF OBAMA-BASHING.

We, the people, the citizens of the United States, get to decide our next president, not the *left-wing media*, not *Hollywood celebrities...*

He is the *least experienced candidate* for president of the United States in at least the last 100 years.

BUT THAT WAS ALL PRELUDE TO THE
MAIN EVENT.

AND MEDIA-BASHING, TOO.

NBC! NBC!

Wooooo! Huhhuhuh!

Very clever.

THE RESULTING "PALIN BOUNCE" HAD PUT MCCAIN **BACK IN THE LEAD.**

ON THE TRAIL, THEY DREW **MASSIVE,** OBAMA-LIKE **CROWDS.**

PALIN EVEN SEEMED **MORE POPULAR** THAN HER RUNNING MATE.

MCCAIN WAS HAPPY TO EXPLOIT HIS NEW WEAPON.

THE GOP CRIED SEXISM.

AND MCCAIN LAUNCHED HIS TOUGHEST ATTACKS YET:

MANY LONGTIME MCCAIN WATCHERS, EVEN PEOPLE WHO USED TO ADMIRE HIM, WERE DISGUSTED.

THE FORMER MILITARY MAN HAD VOWED TO RUN WITH HONOR. BUT HIS CAMPAIGN SEEMED MORE THUGGISH ALL THE TIME AND HE WAS STARTING TO PAY FOR IT.

STILL, MCCAIN WAS DEFINING THE RACE. PEOPLE WERE TALKING ABOUT GENDER, CULTURE, VALUES — NOT THE REAL ISSUES THAT VOTERS WERE SO MAD ABOUT.

IT WAS MCCAIN'S NIGHTMARE.
THE CAMPAIGN WAS NOW ABOUT HIS SINGLE WEAKEST ISSUE: THE ECONOMY. AND HE JUST MADE THINGS WORSE.

GROWING DESPERATE, MCCAIN MADE A DRAMATIC ANNOUNCEMENT.

MCCAIN ALSO CANCELED AN APPEARANCE ON *LETTERMAN.* **BAD MOVE.**

I think someone's putting something in his *Metamucil.*

EVEN THOUGH CONGRESS HADN'T PASSED ITS FINANCIAL BAILOUT BILL, MCCAIN DECIDED TO DEBATE AFTER ALL.

BUT HE WAS CRANKY, UNCOMFORTABLE. WOULDN'T EVEN LOOK OBAMA IN THE EYE.

When the war started, you said it was going to be quick and easy.

OBAMA WAS CLEARLY THE **STRONGER DEBATER.**

You said we knew where the weapons of mass destruction were.

You were wrong.

AS THE ECONOMY MELTED DOWN...

...SO DID THE CULT OF SARAH PALIN.

SARAH THE BARRACUDA WAS BECOMING A PUNCHLINE...

We're gonna ask ourselves, "What would a maverick do in this situation?"...

...and then, you know, we'll do that.

...BUT CONSERVATIVE PUNDITS WEREN'T LAUGHING.

TINA FEY

KATHLEEN PARKER

Palin is obviously not qualified to be president.

She is clearly out of her league. She [should] bow out.

She is a fatal cancer to the Republican Party.

GEORGE WILL

DAVID BROOKS

THE PALIN FIZZLE — AND THE ECONOMY — HAD ROBBED MCCAIN OF HIS FLEETING LEAD.

LEAN OBAMA

LEAN OBAMA

The McCain folks now have to hold every toss-up to stay competitive before they even think about stealing some Obama states.

We are at a tipping point, and if Obama ends up sweeping all of these toss-up states, all of a sudden you're looking at 364 electoral votes.

CHUCK TODD

OBAMA PULLED AHEAD IN VIRGINIA, A STATE DEMOCRATS HADN'T WON SINCE 1964. A TIDE WAS RISING.

AND MCCAIN CAME OFF GRUMPIER THAN EVER.

THE FORMER MEDIA DARLING NOW SEEMED TO HATE REPORTERS.

ANY COLUMNIST WHO WROTE TOO HARSHLY ABOUT HIM
MIGHT WIND UP STRANDED.

THIS WAS NOT
THE HAPPY WARRIOR
OF DAYS PAST.

SOME FRIENDS SAID MCCAIN DIDN'T SEEM LIKE THE SAME MAN
ANYMORE...

BUT FOR OBAMA:

THINGS WERE LOOKING VERY GOOD INDEED.

THE MORE MCCAIN AND PALIN SUNK IN THE POLLS,
THE NASTIER THEY GOT.

Our opponent... is someone who sees America as being so imperfect that he's *palling around with terrorists* who would target their own country.

This is not a man who sees America as you see America and as I see America.

COUNTRY FIRST
JOHN MCCAIN WILL ALWAYS PUT OUR COUNTRY FIRST AS PRE

THE TERRORIST IN QUESTION WAS WILLIAM AYERS, AN ANTI-VIETNAM RADICAL WHO'D HELPED PLAN SOME NON-LETHAL BOMBINGS IN THE 1970S.

WILLIAM AYERS

I don't care about a washed-up terrorist.

WHO IS BARACK OBAMA?

So why are they making their whole campaign about him?

So they can do this.

Obama and
"social circle" in their Hyde
neighborhood. (Chicago tribune,
4/17/08)

Barack Obama. Not Who You Think He Is.

IT SHOULDN'T HAVE BEEN A SURPRISE THAT MCCAIN'S SUPPORTERS RESPONDED IN KIND.

THE FLOODGATES WERE OPEN.

MCCAIN WAS FORCED TO REPUDIATE HIS OWN CORE SUPPORTERS.

THE HEAT OF THE CAMPAIGN WAS NOT GOOD TO MCCAIN. AT EACH DEBATE HE JUST LOOKED WEIRDER.

AND HE WAS PRONE TO SAYING... STRANGE THINGS:

> My fellow *prisoners*...

IN MID-OCTOBER, OBAMA HAD A RUN-IN WITH AN OHIO PLUMBER WORRIED ABOUT HIS TAX PLAN.

> We want to *spread the wealth* around.

MCCAIN SAW A SYMBOL OF THE WHITE AMERICAN MIDDLE-CLASS.

> What you want to do to Joe the Plumber and millions more like him is have their taxes increased and not be able to realize...

> ...the American dream of owning their own business.

NEVER MIND THAT *JOE THE PLUMBER* WASN'T ALL HE WAS CRACKED UP TO BE.

> So let's get this straight. His name is Sam, not Joe. He's not a licensed plumber.

> He doesn't make $250,000 and he would actually benefit from Obama's tax cuts...

> Well, he *didn't...* before he stepped into the national spotlight.

MCCAIN PRACTICALLY BASED HIS CAMPAIGN AROUND THIS UNLIKELY CHARACTER.

JOE THE PLUMBER

> Senator Obama said he wants to *spread the wealth.* My friends, that sounds like *socialism!*

ENJOYING HIS 15-MINUTES OF FAME, REPORTEDLY JOE GOT HIMSELF A RECORD DEAL.

SEEMINGLY UNFAZED, OBAMA KEPT IT STEADY AS SHE GOES, PLAYING THINGS SAFE — AND STUMPING HARD IN RURAL AREAS WHERE DEMOCRATS RARELY GO.

CORINT
BAPTIST CHU

SEN. BARACK OB

RAISING RECORD- SHATTERING AMOUNTS OF MONEY, OBAMA COULD AFFORD TO CLOBBER MCCAIN ON THE AIRWAVES.

$150 million *in September alone??*

Am *I* on the wrong side of the headlines....

Senator Obama's grandmother is gravely ill, and he will be leaving the campaign trail to visit her.

BUT IN THE HEAT OF THE CAMPAIGN, LIFE INTRUDED.

OBAMA HAD THE LUXURY OF LEAVING THE TRAIL BECAUSE THE MCCAIN CAMPAIGN WAS BECOMING SOMETHING OF A JOKE.

PALIN'S ENEMIES WITHIN THE CAMPAIGN LEAKED WORD OF A $150,000 DEPARTMENT STORE SHOPPING SPREE.

I know what a lot of these *elitists* are. The ones that she never went to a *cocktail party* with in Georgetown.

People who think that they can dictate what they believe to America rather than let Americans decide for themselves.

SHE'S GOING *ROGUE!*

DIVA!

BUT SOME OF THE NASTIEST SHOTS CAME FROM WITHIN HIS OWN CAMPAIGN.

WHAT A WHACK JOB...

HOCKEY MOM.

IN THE CLOSING DAYS, RACE HUNG OVER THE CAMPAIGN LIKE A SHADOW.

A REPORTED POLITICAL ATTACK BY A BLACK MAN CAUSED A BRIEF SENSATION.

FOLLOWED BY DISGUST OVER THE SICK HOAX.

TO HIS CREDIT, MCCAIN RESISTED ADVISORS URGING HIM TO DROP THE JEREMIAH WRIGHT BOMB.

No.

BUT CODED ATTACKS CONTINUED NATIONWIDE.

DOZENS OF CALL-CENTER **WORKERS ASKED TO MAKE NASTY CALLS** ABOUT OBAMA'S RECORD OF "CODDLING CRIMINALS" WALKED OFF THE JOB.

RACIAL PREJUDICE STILL EXISTED,

BUT IT COULDN'T COMPETE WITH THE OBAMA TIDAL WAVE.

MCCAIN INSISTED THE RACE WAS CLOSE. BUT THE POLLS TOLD AN UNDENIABLE STORY.

ELECTION DAY

FINAL POLLS WERE SOLID.

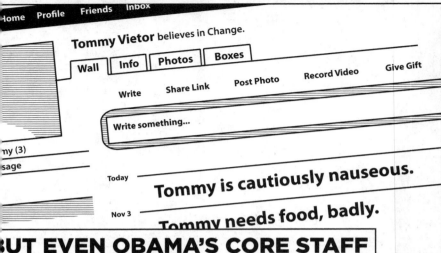

Home   Profile   Friends   Inbox

Tommy Vietor believes in Change.

Wall | Info | Photos | Boxes

Write   Share Link   Post Photo   Record Video   Give Gift

Write something...

...my (3)

...sage

Today

Tommy is cautiously nauseous.

Nov 3

Tommy needs food, badly.

BUT EVEN OBAMA'S CORE STAFF COULDN'T BE SURE OF THE RESULTS.

They just called Pennsylvania for Obama; it's over.

IT WASN'T LONG BEFORE THE OUTCOME BECAME CLEAR.

Here at Obama HQ, people are openly weeping tears of joy.

AND THEN:

...t in: ...orting ...a has ...equisite ...otes.

Barack Obama is the *44th president of the United States.*

FOR SOME, IT WAS THE SWAN SONG OF THE **CIVIL RIGHTS MOVEMENT.**

FOR OTHERS, PROOF THAT HISTORY **HAD LEFT THEM BEHIND.**

MCCAIN ACCEPTED HIS BITTER DEFEAT WITH GRACE:

SARAH HUSSEIN OBAMA

HARLEM

APO

HIS WORDS WERE HEARD

米大統領誕生

OBAMA

OBAMA, JAPAN

AROUND THE WORLD.